CW00539536

THE ALFA ROMEO TRADITION

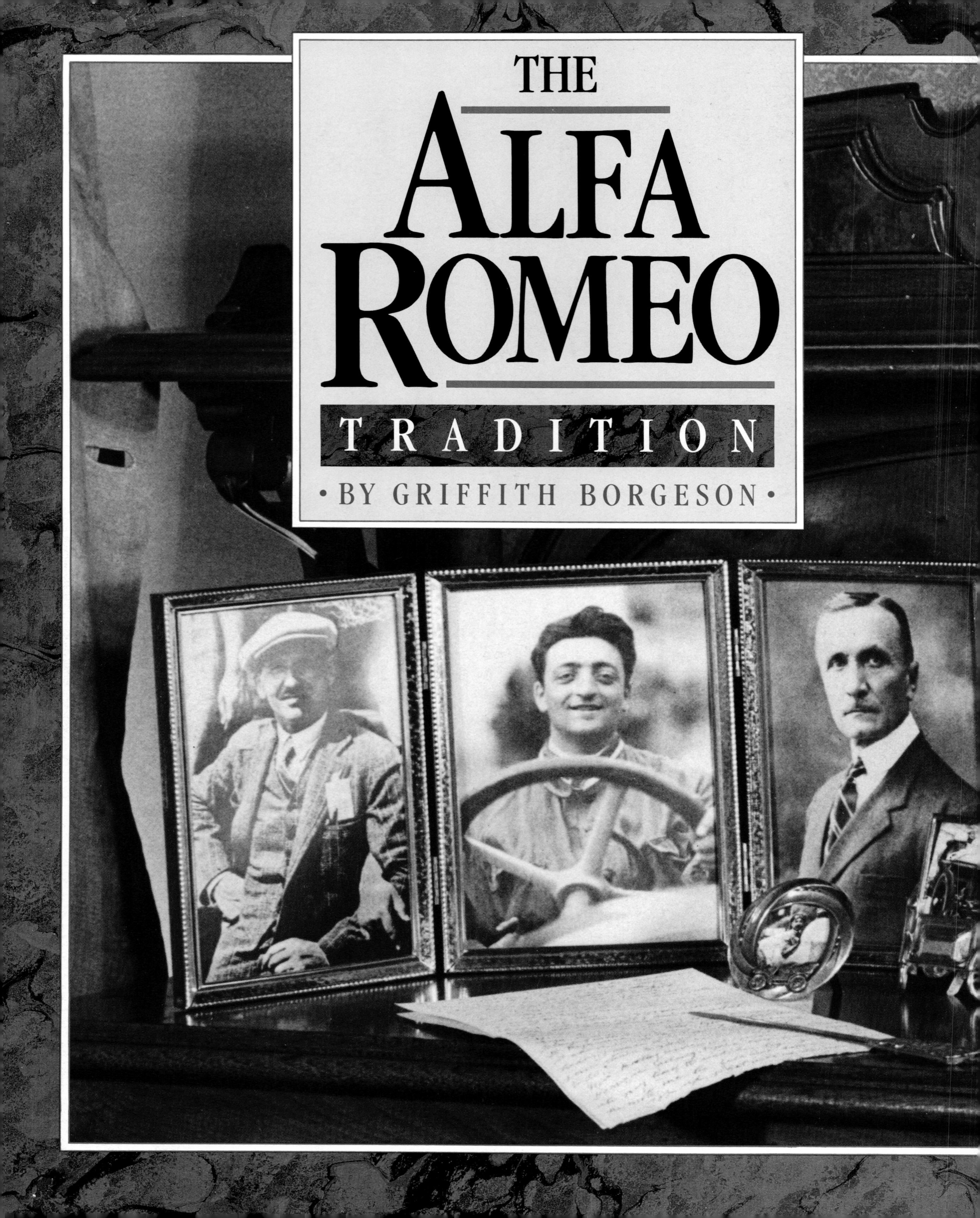
THE
ALFA
ROMEO
TRADITION
•BY GRIFFITH BORGESON•

16
Foulis
Haynes

CONTENTS

A **FOULIS** Motoring Book

ISBN 0-85429-875-4

First published 1990

This edition published by:
Haynes Publishing Group
Sparkford, Nr Yeovil, Somerset, BA22 7JJ.
England

Produced by Automobile Quarterly, Inc.
420 North Park Road
Wyomissing, PA 19610-2918, USA

President: Glenn F. Johns
Editor for this book: Julie Fenster
Book Design: Michael Pardo and Jean Seibert
Editorial Assistant: Vivian Einsel

Printing and typesetting by Kutztown Publishing Company, Inc.,
Kutztown, Pennsylvania

Binding by National Publishing Company, Inc.
Philadelphia, Pennsylvania

Color Separations by Red Rose Graphics, Ltd.
Lancaster, Pennsylvania

DEDICATION

The unique Alfa Romeo mystique grew out of cars which were created by men. It is probably impossible to think of any marque in history whose personnel roster has contained such a mass of distinguished names. Yet, while the literature of Alfa cars is richly abundant, that of the creators and original protagonists of the marque's history is less than scant. Here we seek to do honor to some of the more outstanding of these personages.

But in essence, this book is dedicated to each member of that elite group which, with devotion, pride and skill, contributed to the creation of the Alfa tradition which survives so strongly today.

Romeo

CHAPTER 1

GIUSEPPE MEROSI

Giuseppe Merosi
1872-1956
Technical Director

"EVERY TIME I SEE an Alfa Romeo pass by, I raise my hat'' Henry Ford once said. It would be interesting to know which breed of Alfa the great industrialist had in mind. The tradition of Giuseppe Merosi was one of solid, slow-revving conservatism, whereas a decade later, Vittorio Jano practically invented that of the high-spirited and agile thoroughbred Italian light car.

The Merosi strain was born with the Alfa company. That firm traced its origins to the founding of the Societá Anonima Italiana Darracq at Naples in 1906, and its move to Milan the following year. This assembler of French hardware went bankrupt in 1909, when its assets were taken over by a new group of investors. Letting the word *societá* be understood, they named their company the Anonima Lombarda Fabbrica Automobili. From a very early date the initials A.L.F.A. were also written ALFA and Alfa. The acronym, with the sound of the first letter of the Greek alphabet, evoked a dawn-like image of beginning, of newness, and of promise for the future. It was this nascent firm, in the process of getting organized, which engaged Merosi in October 1909 to be its technical director, to design a pair of new cars, and to oversee their production. His job became official with the constitution of the new, all-Italian corporation on January 1, 1910.

Aside from what can be deduced from his work, practically all that we know about Merosi we owe to historians Luigi Fusi and Angelo Tito Anselmi. Fusi worked under the old engineer for years, and Anselmi has known members of Merosi's immediate family for a similar period. The fact that so little has been recoverable, in spite of these seemingly fertile situations, forces the conclusion that Merosi was an extremely private person, even toward his intimates.

This page. Right: Young Merosi. Below: Merosi (in front passenger seat) with his first passenger car, a 1900 O & M 5HP. Opposite page: 1910 24 HP, by Castagna, owned by the Alfa Romeo Museo.

It is known that he was born in Piacenza, about forty miles southeast of Milan on the south shore of the River Po, on December 17, 1872. His mother was born Anna Pavesi and his father, Giacomo, had a small candle-manufacturing business. The family enjoyed rather affluent middle-class status and was able to put Giuseppe through the city's technical institute, from which he emerged with the title of *Geometra* (Surveyor). He would be called *Geometra Merosi* for the rest of his life.

The young college graduate was handsome and well-built, standing an exceptional six-feet-one-inch tall. He is said to have had a friendly disposition, but one that was tempered by great modesty. This could be a way of expressing the fact that he was extremely shy and reticent. He was a good athlete, loved cycling and did well as a bicycle racer, although there is no suggestion that he was of championship timber. He seems to have shunned the parental candle works, and a document exists which testifies to his having worked very well as a surveyor for the state department of public thoroughfares. Somewhere around 1895, at about age twenty-three, Merosi obtained the money from his family that enabled him to go into business with a friend, engineer Vittorio Bassi. According to the local press, the widely travelled Bassi had been technical director of the Gladiator cycle factory in Paris for two years. By early 1897 the firm of Ing. Bassi & Merosi was being hailed for the excellence of the bicycles which it manufactured under the fashionably English trade name of "Endless."

Then comes a gap in the story which ends in 1899, with the firm of Orio & Marchand moving from the outskirts of Milan to Piacenza. This company manufactured sewing machines and motorcycles and was at work on its first car, which turned out to have much in common with the French Decauville. Anselmi states that Merosi left his own little company in order to join O&M as a demonstrator and tester. He took part in motorcycle races in which O&M machines were top performers, and very quickly was promoted to the position of chief designer. Where and when he had acquired the qualifications for that post is another blank in the story. Once installed, his experience may have snowballed. These turn-of-the-century years brought the birth of the Italian automotive industry. The record book of the Automobile Club d'Italia shows that O&M, and then March and without Orio, were very active in racing at this period. This would have submitted Merosi to the conditioning which that discipline alone can provide.

There is documentation to show that, around 1905, Merosi did a stint of perhaps a year with Fiat in Turin. Then, in 1906, he is said to have taken over as head of the automotive (as opposed to the bicycle) engineering department of the Edoardo Bianchi company in Milan. It was perhaps on the stroke of this success that he wed a girl with the sonorous name of Adalgisa Malvezzi. There are also indications that it was at this time that his association began with Antonio Santoni, a fellow automobilist and trained surveyor, who would subsequently resurface at Alfa as a top aide. It is stated that Merosi was personally responsible for all or most of the design of all Bianchi cars from 1907 through 1909, including the marque's first shaft-drive chassis, which was released early in 1910.

Right: Merosi at the wheel of Alfa's first production model, the 24 HP. Below right: 1911 12/15HP chassis. Part of the original Alfa product line-up, it was a scaled-down version of the 24HP.

Bianchi was then a large and important manufacturer, and one must wonder how, in a market glutted with qualified engineers, Geometra Merosi had acquired the experience and skills that would permit him to arrive at such a coveted and demanding position. We know not, but we know his subsequent performance, and it leaves not the shadow of a doubt that this self-trained automotive engineer had attained a high level of competence in his chosen field. It sufficed to bring to him the directors of the Alfa company-to-be.

The L-head valve layout had just begun to replace the T-head in the Italian industry and it was that strictly up-to-date configuration that Merosi used in his engines for Alfa's first two models, the 4084 cc 24 HP and the 2413 cc 12HP, both of which made their bow that year. The chassis and power plants of these two were thoroughly and safely conventional, differing from their peers only in petty nuances of design. They were honest products of good quality, and the company sought to popularize them through participation in an occasional speed event, in which success was slow in coming. It was immediate, however, in the field of aviation and came about this way:

Santoni joined Darracq Italiana early in 1909, probably as a draftsman. Shortly thereafter he invented a mechanically-driven centrifugal supercharger for automobile-type engines. He filed for an Italian patent on this remarkable bit of pioneering on June 1 and it was granted on March 14 of the following year.

Santoni had a good friend named Nino Franchini who, in 1908, had been prominent as a racing driver of Bianchi cars — a documented fact which suggests that this pair and Merosi had known each other at this period, if not earlier. Aviation was just aborning in Italy, as elsewhere, and in the fall of 1909 Santoni and Franchini had an idea for the

design of a more stable type of aircraft. Santoni made the calculations and began laying out its design that November. It seemed so promising to Alfa managing director Ugo Stella that, early in January, he authorized the construction of a prototype.

This decision was made with the new Merosi 24 HP engine in mind. Its design had been completed before Alfa had come into official being and the first run of three units was in an advanced stage of fabrication. Cavalier Stella assigned one of these engines to the aircraft project, and it was submitted to every possible weight-reducing measure.

Most of the historical details surrounding Alfa's foray into aviation are drawn from an eight-page, single-space typescript on the subject, which Santoni himself wrote and signed in 1941, and which I had the luck to stumble upon recently in an unlikely corner of the company's archives. Santoni does not go into detail concerning the problems which had to be overcome before his partner put the Santoni-Franchini biplane into the air. It may well have taken time to find out that 24 bhp was not enough to do the job.

Above: The Alfa-engined airplane prototype on its first flight, September 17, 1910. Left: Franchini at the controls of the plane. Far left: The 24HP engine, one of the first three made, as prepared for the aircraft. Note the lightweight wire steel-spoke flywheel. The supercharger was yet to be installed.

In the end, the Santoni supercharger was applied to Merosi's engine, enabling it to produce 36 bhp at 1680 rpm, and enabling it to fly, on September 17, 1910, in the presence of a group of company officials.

The plane, one of the earliest all-Italian ones to work, did so well that it was purchased by a Milan flying school. The Alfa management decided to concentrate its resources on automotive production, though, and left further aeronautical pioneering to others. Franchini settled into being the firm's chief test driver, as well as its top competition pilot on the side. Merosi continued as technical director, and Santoni became head of the design department and Merosi's second in command, taking full charge in his absence. Giulio Ramponi, who had the greatest esteem for both men, told me that, during the Merosi era, ''some of the design ideas came from Merosi, and some from Santoni. They worked as a team.'' After Merosi left Alfa, Santoni joined Isotta Fraschini in a highly placed engineering capacity. Franchini became the marque's agent in Trento, just north of Lake Garda.

1913 40/60HP Corsa, owned by the Alfa Romeo Museo. This original chassis carries a rebuilt body dating from 1920.

sation was its greatly augmented power output, from 49 to 67 bhp. This thirty-seven percent improvement was obtained through a higher compression ratio, altered valve timing, a side-draft carburetor and a symbolic 166 cc increase in piston displacement. The power peak now occurred at 2600 rather than 2400 rpm. Although the Series E chassis had been shortened by a whole foot to make the ES, it was heavier and more rigid. With a specific power output that was far higher than that of any previous Alfa (other than the GP prototype), the ES began to hack out a respectable racing reputation for itself. Enzo Ferrari had joined the firm as a *uomo di tutto fare* and it was on stripped ES chassis that he began his competition career with Alfa in 1921. His teammates were Antonio Ascari and Ugo Sivocci. Between their exploits and those of a growing number of sportsmen and sportswomen, who were drawn to the marque by the ES, the Alfa performance image began to glow and become known worldwide.

In his book, *Tutte le Vetture Alfa Romeo dal 1910*, Luigi Fusi says that the next model, the Tipo G1, was "based on the design of the American and British cars of the time." Enzo Ferrari, in his *Le Mie Gioie Terribili*, describes the G1 as being "derived from an American machine brought expressly from the U.S.A. in order to examine the postwar

MEROSI ENGINES

	L-HEAD 4C	L-HEAD 6C	OHV 4C	OHV 6C	DOHC 4C	DOHC 6C
1910	24 HP 100mm x 130mm — 12, 15 HP 80 x 120					
1913			40-60 110 x 160			
1914					1914 GP 100 x 143	
1921	20-30 ES 102 x 130	G1 98 x 140			1914 GP REVISED 100 x 143	
1922				RL, RLS 75 x 110 76 x 110		
1923			RM 75 x 110	RL TF 78 x 110		P1 65 x 100
1924				RL TF 80 x 120		

Above left: chart shows the development of the Merosi era. Above right: The Merosi children in the original 1910 24HP prototype, August 7, 1910. Below right: The 1910 24HP motor.

realizations of the great transatlantic makes." In their booklet, *The Type RL Alfa Romeos*, Peter Hull and Fusi recount an inverted sequence of events: "In order to get an insight into American production methods, Alfa Romeo acquired a Pierce-Arrow car before bringing out their next model." That statement is echoed by Maurice Hendry in "Pierce Arrow, An American Aristocrat" (*Automobile Quarterly*, Volume VI, Number 3). For what it may be worth, the G1 and 1920 Pierce-Arrow Series 31 both were sixes. And, although the Italian engine's stroke was the smaller by a quarter of an inch, both happened to have identical bores. The Pierce, in spite of its four valves per cyclinder, was an archaic T-head, while the 6.3-liter Alfa was, quite simply, a scaled-up version of its inhouse L-head predecessors. It is doubtful that Pierce at that time had any design ideas that Alfa would care to use. Alfa's interest in that noble American marque more probably lay in the analysis of its very high quality of workmanship and finish as achieved through the use of machine, rather than hand, methods.

TIPO RL

Alfa's management recognized the necessity of producing a genuinely modern postwar product, and its design progressed in parallel with that of the G1 in 1920. This was the Tipo RL, according to Fusi, conceived as a touring machine that would be adaptable to racing under the three-liter formula which would come into effect the following year. That formula, of course, would apply to thoroughbreds of Grand Prix calibre, not dual-purpose cars, all of which would show up at Le Mans in July 1921 with at least a single overhead camshaft. But perhaps Alfa's intent was not as naive as this rationale would make it seem. Perhaps it was a shrewd decision to be *á la mode* that prompted management to put its money on the combination of pushrod valve operation with the piston displacement that would be shared by the world's most avant-garde vehicles. Ballot used that strategy during the subsequent two-liter formula.

The engine which Merosi designed for his RL series, along with bringing much success and fame to the marque, had its original if not folkloric aspects. It was a six with pressurized oil supplied to its four plain main bearings. Its vertical overhead valves formed a single file down the cyl-

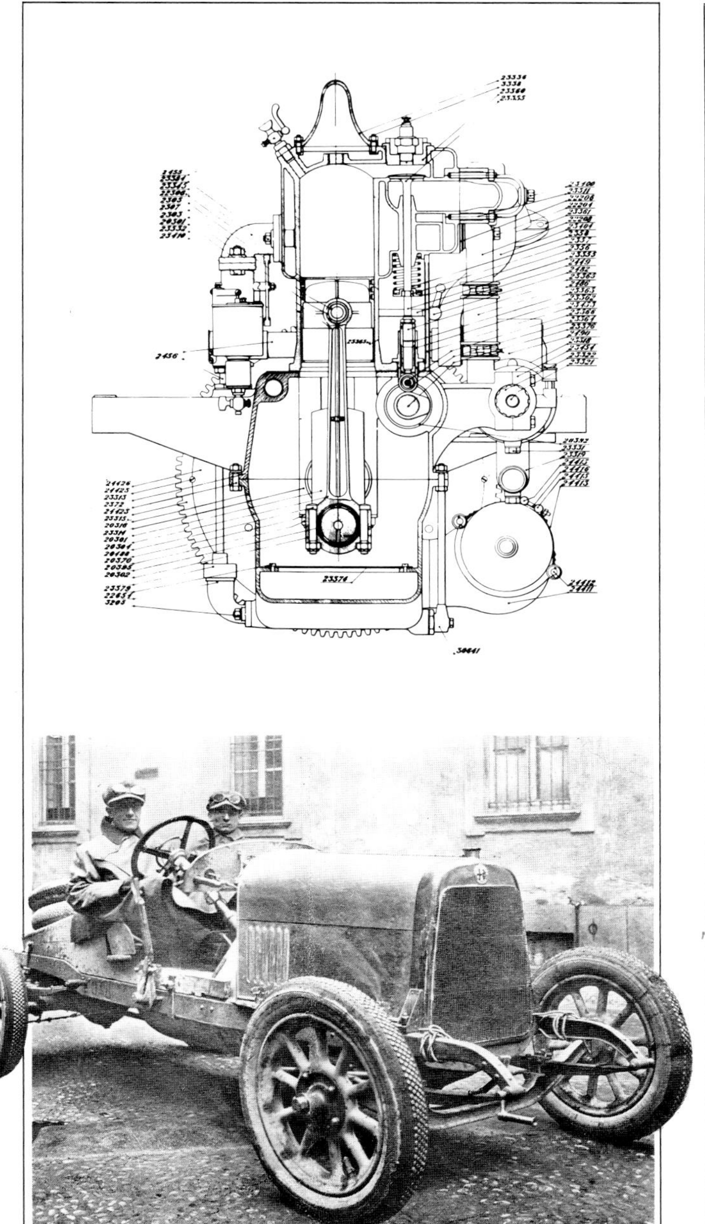

Clockwise from left, below: 1921 20/30HP chassis, undergoing testing with Montalbani and Boni; the 1920 20/30HP engine; Merosi at the wheel a 1924 RM, August 15, 1924; the 1924 RM engine.

inders' centerline. The valve heads were flush with the gasket face of the detachable cylinder head, which was perfectly flat, all of the combustion space being contained in the cylinder proper. The rocker arms were desirably short, and each valve was closed by a pair of concentric coil springs. Each pushrod worked against a large coil spring all of its own — presumably a precaution against floating of the valve gear, but one which swallowed its share of horsepower. They were Merosi's mark, like his "brake-shoe" rocker springs on the old Tipo 40-60. Peter Hull remarked that the pushrods "were surprisingly heavy, and a spare one would be perfectly suitable for keeping beside the bed for attacking burglars." Automatic lubrication of the valve gear was not provided for, felt pads under the rocker cover having to be soaked by hand at frequent intervals. Adjusting the valve lash was a two-man job — one man to handle the feeler gauge between the rocker arm and valve stem, and another on the other side of the car to adjust the tappets at the base of the pushrods.

The basic model was the RLN, the *Normale*, with bore and stroke of 75 x 110 mm. Then came the *Sport* model, the RLS, with an extra millimeter of bore that made no meaningful contribution to output but which certainly complicated the manufacturing process annoyingly and wastefully. In the same spirit, the exhaust and inlet sides were on the left and right respectively on the *Normale* and the opposite on the *Sport*. It was a clean and handsome engine, and it exceeded by far the specific output of all prior Alfas (again with the exception of the figures for the no-show 1914 GP car).

The one or more RL's that were introduced in Milan in October 1921 were merely prototypes. Six cars were made in 1922, and it was not until '23 that real production began, with front-wheel brakes becoming standard in September

of that year. The cars, including the sports models, also were by far the heaviest that Alfa had yet made, the *Normale* easily weighing two tons wet. The RLS and SS, only about 100 pounds lighter, nevertheless did wonderfully as campaigned by the factory racing team of Ascari, Campari, Ferrari and Sivocci, to the greater glory of the marque. Then in 1923 and '24 Merosi produced very light, short chassis to receive high-compression, high-revving versions of his new engine. These constituted the Targa Florio models, called RL TF, which were almost fifty percent lighter than any of the production RL's. They boasted dry-sump lubrication, seven main bearings instead of the usual four, dual carburetors, and output of up to 125 bhp rather than the 56 of the *Normale*. The TF's manifestly were rather good racing machines, ponderous pushrods and all, and they began to make Alfa not only an important factor on the national scale, but to make an impression internationally, beginning with first, second and fourth and top lap time in the 1923 Targa Florio.

Idiosyncrasies and all, the RL was a reliable and lovable car that could perform fairly spectacularly. It handled extraordinarily well. It is widely referred to as "Merosi's masterpiece."

Back in 1920, when Merosi was well occupied with the development of his pushrod six, he had another go at unlocking the potential which certainly should have been present in his 1914 twin-cam GP engine. He redesigned its top end radically. Hoping for more efficient filling of its cy-

linders, he abandoned the old straight-through porting in favor of a gooseneck form which would direct the fuel/air mixture down into the barrels, instead of across their tops. By one of those unlikely coincidences which are so commonplace, Fiat adopted the same idea at about the same time — obviously it was in the professional air. Thus, Merosi appears to have the distinction of being the co-originator of this hallmark of Italian high-performance engine design. It did him no good, however. Ironically, in spite of all the right stuff, he never got really close to the bhp/liter figure of his own pushrod RLS. Still, this second GP car was raced nine times between 1919 and 1921, driven by Franchini, Campari and Ascari to two firsts, a third and five did-not-finishes.

Fusi credits Nicola Romeo with the conception of the RM line: a two-liter four to be assembled largely from components of the RL series. The clean little engine appeared to be mainly of aluminum but, like the equally handsome RL, it had a cast-iron cylinder head. Specific output compared very well with that of the sixes, but while engine size and total power output had been reduced by about a third, weight was reduced by only about fifteen percent. An RM weighed about 70 to 85 pounds per bhp dry and, when fuelled up and ready to go, it was pitifully underpowered. The line, introduced in 1923, was retired in 1926.

While Merosi's RL's would go on enhancing his and Alfa's reputation for years to come, his star set for good with his third and final try at a full-race engine, known as the P1. In the fall of 1922, aided as always by Santoni, he went to work on a twin-cam six for the two-liter formula then in force. With built-up steel cylinders and a full roller-bearing lower end, it was a perfectly straightforward derivation from the current Fiat GP 804. Like Merosi's former twin-cam efforts, this one could not be made to produce a state-of-the-art power output, and even supercharging failed to help.

The designer of these costly failures was given other responsibilities, while a promising young designer was brought in to work under him.

On top of the P1 debacle, the demand for three-liter production cars withered away. Then someone in the production department increased the speed with which the holes for RL's valve guides were bored, and a catastrophic num-

Opposite page: 1921 RL SS, by Castagna, originally ordered for an Indian maharajah, owned by the Alfa Romeo Museo. This page, left: 1921 Tipo G1 and a detail from an advertising piece for the 20-30 ES.

Clockwise from right: Antonietta Avanzo with her 20/30 ES race car at Brescia, 1921; another 1921 20/30 ES gathers urchins and on-lookers on the street; the twin-cam six, two-liter P1 motor; Sivocci at the wheel of a 1923 P1, he was later killed in an accident in this car.

ber of cylinder heads had to be scrapped.

Merosi supported his declining fortunes until early 1926, when he is said to have voluntarily resigned. Subsequent letters from him to Alfa's management expressed his regret at having taken this action and his desire for reinstatement. Then, in mid-1929, he signed a contract with Mathis of Strasbourg, where he appears to have worked as a consultant for a year or two. In 1931 he was back in Italy, as chief designer for the Frera motorcycle company of Tradate, near Varese. Nineteen thirty-six found him back in Milan, heading the truck department at Isotta Fraschini. There, he drew up a proposed new car for IF, an all-independently sprung luxury six. The design is pictured and discussed in detail on page 192 of Anselmi's *Isotta Fraschini*. There, in a longitudinal section of the engine, one recognizes the thick pushrods of the RL, complete with

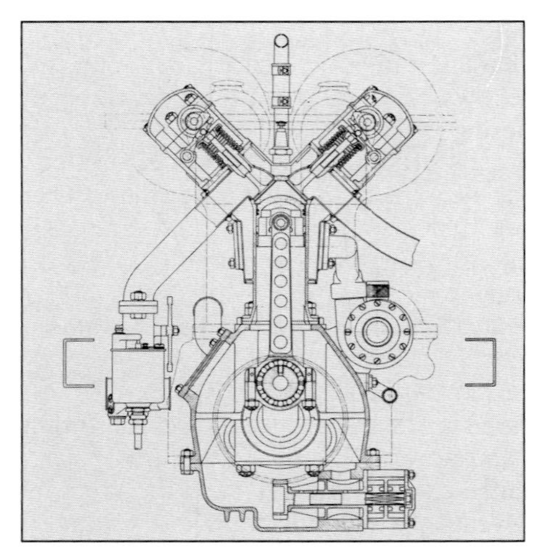

Left: Merosi at the wheel of a 1923 RM at Torino. Below: Cavalier Merosi at the age of 84.

their curious, characteristically Merosi coil springs. Whether this project was an assignment from the company or a voluntary offering is unclear.

Aside from Merosi's death in 1956, at age eighty-four, the story that I was able to piece together ended there. Then one day in October 1985 I was listening to a retired Alfa executive, Dr. Antonio Bearzotti, reminisce about his career. He had started with the company in 1935, at age fifteen. At age twenty, he said, he worked for two years at the side of . . . Cavalier Merosi. *Who*? That's right; none other than the designer of the first Alfas.

Merosi had suffered terrible financial reverses, according to my informant, and was broke. He went to Alfa Romeo and asked to be taken back on the payroll. In spite of the fact that he was seventy, he was given a job as a designer in the industrial vehicle division. When other, younger designers would run into a stone wall, the division heads would say, ''Let's go see Cavalier Merosi.'' A typical example was the conversion of the firm's dual-axle military trucks into tracklayers for the North African theater of World War II. The draftsman to whom the job was assigned agonized over it for weeks without finding a workable solution. So it was handed to Merosi, who found the mechanical solution and laid the whole thing out in a shade over twenty days. Young Bearzotti begged to give a hand with the detailing but the old man just laughed and said that he could work faster all by himself. Working on a huge upright drawing board, he would lay out his key points. Then he would draw all of his horizontal lines. With those done, he would draw all of his vertical lines *zip, zip, zip* — and then tie it all together. ''Along with being absolutely brilliant, he worked with incredible speed. I never saw anything like it before or since. A true phenomenon. And the stories that he remembered about the old days!'' Merosi liked to describe himself as the ''founder'' of Alfa Romeo. In a way, he was.

Beazotti left to do his hitch in the Army. When he returned to his job, old Geometra Merosi was gone.

CHAPTER 2

NICOLA ROMEO

Nicola Romeo
1876-1938
Managing Director

IN THE SPACE of a handful of years Nicola Romeo, starting with a small shop employing about 50 workers, built his business into one of the most prominent industrial complexes in Italy. His name itself became the household word which it remains today, and he moved in the highest financial and political circles. Reading the story of his business career, which is masterfully recorded in historian Duccio Bigazzi's 663-page tome, *Il Portello* (1988), one is constantly reminded of his American empire-building counterpart Billy Durant, who formed General Motors. Both were men of the most daring vision and courage, both were victims of almost pathological optimism and both were incapable of running the empires they created. A liability for both men was the incapacity to delegate authority to men who could have done better. Both were giants with feet of clay. A certain intimate glimpse of Romeo's personality is given us by his granddaughter Daniela Romeo Maestri, in an article by Manuela Piscini in *Ruoteclassiche* magazine for June 1989. She says:

> He was an extremely lovable person, kind, but with a very remarkable charisma which inspired a sort of reverent fear in his human contacts. A composite personality: on one hand generosity, imagination, approachability, the ability to laugh at himself; on the other hand, technological rigor, the will to study, to be meticulously precise. Even within the family he required a reasonable deference [on the part of its members toward him]. The family, however, was, along with his work, his greatest love. All of his free time was for his seven children, four boys and three girls. He had a mate who was extraordinarily intelligent: Donna Angelina Valadin, a Portuguese. From the letters which I have found, it seems that the two loved each other very much. Grandmother Angelina

Right: An electric trolley, ca. 1920, typical of production at the Rome plant. Nicola Romeo is seated at the window, slightly to the right of the numerals "715." Below: General Marone visiting the Alfa Romeo plant at Portello in 1916.

was a stupendous mistress of the house, a woman of rare determination. And I can say that from direct knowledge because she was for me a guide in more than one moment of my life. A fundamental presence for *il nonno* [Grandpa], a mate in the most modern sense of the term.

It is interesting that, in the opening sentence of this sentimental portrait, Daniela Maestri underlines the hard, fear-inspiring side of her grandfather's character. He did not look the part of one of his country's leading captains of industry. He was short, bald, bushily moustached and often looked as though he had just stepped out of a Hal Roach comedy. Having the capacity to laugh at himself, he frequently played a comic role for public consumption, particularly when faced by a camera. But behind the often pixie-ish façade was the empire-builder's indomitable will. On the surface he was low-key, and in the business world he was known as "The Siren," in recognition of his seductive powers of persuasion. All of the major decisions concerning the operation of his far-flung activities came from him. But he had partners—private investors and banks—who maintained at least a public silence, but whose will was not to be ignored. He founded the parent company and absorbed others which already existed. Romeo played to the hilt the role of owner of it all but, in reality, he was just another stockholder, and one all-too-often in mortal debt to the bankers.

entitled to 35 percent of the net profits in excess of the six percent earmarked for interest on capital. As Bigazzi notes, this did a great deal for Romeo's personal fortune.

Figures on wartime profits of the company (prior to its incorporation as a public company) were very private information, but merited well the adjective "fabulous." After the incorporation in 1918, the declared earnings for that year were only slightly over $800,000, which was still not bad. But postwar excess-profits investigations—in which Merosi testified against the company—brought many undeclared pots of gold to light.

A government program for the mechanization of national agriculture led Romeo in 1918 to undertake the manufacture of American Titan tractors under license. With 350 built, when they were put on the market the following year they found virtually no buyers. Money was made, nevertheless, from the railway sector and from steel structural members, adding up to a profit of $264,368 for 1919.

It is striking that automobiles formed no part of this initial reconversion program. Automotive production—totally alien to Romeo's background—came as an afterthought, if not as a sort of last resort, the program starting in late July of 1919. Good automotive engineers were hard to find, and Merosi had severed connections with the company on May 1918 over having been exiled to one of its southern rail factories. He had even taken legal action against La Romeo. His talents were certainly missed during the tractor fiasco, an uneasy peace was made, and he was brought back to Il Portello, but, according to Bigazzi, only in the rather tentative capacity of Technical Consultant. Much costly reconversion was essential in order to render one of the factory buildings suitable for building cars. Output be-

Above: The RL SS takes the winner's lap at Avus in the 1926 GP of Germany. Left: pillars of Romeo's great racing teams, Ferrari, Ascari and Campari.

Alfa roadsters. Left lower: 1925 RL SS by Castagna; left upper: 1921 ES Tipo Sport; center: a 1926 RL SS; right, upper: 1926 RL SS by Zagato; right, lower: 1927 6C 1500.

gan with the assembly of parts left over from prewar days, which is what the competition was doing. This permitted the sale of about 105 15-20, 20-30 and 40-50 models by the end of 1920. For the first time, the name of Romeo joined that of Alfa on the trademark and badges of the company's automotive division.

In the meanwhile, Merosi had thoroughly redesigned and greatly improved the prewar 20-30, resulting in the sporting 20-30 ES which was introduced in 1921. According to the company publication, *Conoscere l'Alfa Romeo* (Arese, 1983), "The automobile was not to represent the most important product of the firm, but was to constitute its image, summing up its [various] products." The ES, seen only in prototype form in 1920, set the quality-combined-with-performance theme which characterized the marque from this time onward. Nicola Romeo's personal conveyance at this time became a standard 20-30 with an elegant town car body, in which the chauffeur sat in the open, but with a permanent roof over his head. The year 1920 was a disastrous one for Italy in general. For one thing, the bottom almost fell out of the lira. Suddenly it cost 21 lire to buy a dollar, and any other hard currency was just as dear. The cost of imported raw materials, manufactured goods and petroleum products became relatively prohibitive. Great amounts of new capital were needed, and that of La Romeo was increased to 60 million lire. Due to the devaluation which had taken place, this impressive figure was worth only $2.84 million and was quite inadequate to the needs of the company, which were augmented by uncontrolled expansion. Canestrini stated that adequate and rational organization was lacking throughout the sprawling corporation. At the end of 1920, La Romeo owed the BIS very close to 90 million lire ($4,257,000). Earnings for the year were about $160,000.

That put La Romeo second on the long list of BIS debtors, headed by Ansaldo, which owed 700 million lire. To cover its own galloping insolvency at this time the BIS began borrowing large amounts from other institutions, and they soon reached a total of 1.76 billion lire, about $72 million. Finally the BIS closed its doors for good on December 30, 1921. In his memoirs Enzo Ferrari remembered the bursting of the BIS bubble as one of the great politico-financial scandals of the era. But it was just one of the catastrophic incidents that precipitated a state of almost

constant crisis in Italian industry and the widespread breakdown of the country's banking system and economy in general. On April 9, 1922, the Government took the unprecedented step of creating, through its central bank, the Banca Nazionale di Credito (BNC), chiefly to supervise and manage the ponderous liquidation of the BIS. This entailed attempted salvage operations within the companies that were most heavily in debt to the BIS. This, and not the takeover of La Romeo by the Institute for Industrial Reconstruction (IRI) in 1933, marked the beginning of the Government's takeover of the derelict company. At the outset it was unobtrusive, sought only to guide, and interfered minimally with Romeo's conduct of his business. But gentle persuasion was ineffective.

Although prototypes of Merosi's finest creation, the RL, had been seen earlier, production began in 1923. It was an excellent car and it set a company record of 829 sales that year, which still failed to get the books out of the red. Unfortunately, RL sales were down in 1924, in spite of the P2 victory at Lyon, but the unloading of various properties and a new aero-engine contract raised receipts to a postwar high of 3,768,900 lire (about $164,000). The BNC, however, had taken control, and Nicola Romeo's title of board chairman had little meaning left. During that year the Government bank first sold off the locomotive factory at Saronno, followed by the rolling stock properties in Rome and Naples.

ROMEO LOSES CONTROL

In June 1925 Alfa Romeo won the Belgian GP, followed by the French GP a month later. On the team's return to Milan, Prime Minister Mussolini personally had their procession showered with flowers from military planes. When Alfa won the newly created World Championship of road racing at Monza in September, Il Duce's official car ceased to be a Fiat and became an Alfa, which he openly referred to as "the best national product." On the 21st of October the Board of the company voted to quit racing and to invest that enormous budget in the regular production program. The image which Romeo had sought to achieve for his marque had been acquired and, for the present, there was nothing left to prove.

La Domenica Sportiva

SETTIMANALE ILLUSTRATO de "La Gazzetta dello Sport"

Anno XII - N. 27 | 5 Luglio 1925 | Cent. 50 la copia

L'industria automobilistica italiana per merito dell'Alfa-Romeo e di Antonio Ascari conferma a Spa, come a Lione e a Monza, un indiscusso primato mondiale.

L'arrivo trionfale dei Vittoriosi a Milano. — Antonio Ascari (a sinistra) - Il Gr. Uff. Nicola Romeo (al centro) - A destra: Giuseppe Campari

Above, Romeo with Ascari and Campari at Monza, October, 1924. Below: A detail from an advertising piece of 1924, by the artist Magritte

However, the State-owned bank which was charged with minimizing the damage done by the BIS had long since decided that Romeo was categorically incapable of running an organization of this magnitude and was determined to eliminate him from the overall equation. At first the bank sought an executive who would work alongside Romeo and systematically strip him of his remaining grip on the company. Nobody wanted the hypocritical job. Then, at a Board meeting on March 22, 1925, the bank maneuvered to dismiss Ojetti as president, to ''promote'' Romeo laterally into that position, and to assign his former managerial functions to a committee of its own choosing.

Then came the Board meeting of December 31, 1925, which was one of the most decisive turning points in Romeo's life and in the history of Alfa Romeo. On that oc-

casion it was formally decreed that henceforth the firm would concentrate solely on automotive production and sales, along with engines for aircraft. Adventures in railroading and elsewhere were finished. And, since the BNC's committee had been ineffectual in dislodging the Romeo management from power, the bank had continued to search for a strong man who could handle the job. He was found in the person of Ing. Pasquale Gallo who, over the violent protests of the Old Guard, was made managing director of La Romeo.

Gallo was a Meridionale, a man of the south, himself, and he was in his element crossing swords with Romeo's exclusively southern High Command. Gallo was born in Bari, in 1887. He had gone north to Turin, where he obtained his degree in mechanical engineering at that city's famous Polytechnic. He was a brilliant young man who, in 1913 and at the age of 26, became the technical director of an important Torinese manufacturing firm. He made such a name for himself that, in 1922, the newly created BNC engaged him to attempt the resurrection of Automobili Itala, another name on the list of flotsam left by the wreckage of the BIS. He got that company back on its feet, whereupon the BNC prevailed upon him to take on a much more serious and near-hopeless case: La Romeo. It was Gallo against the entrenched Old Guard and he broke it down, man by man.

Gallo had an iron will, a clear-cut plan, and draconian methods. He made it clear that he would save the company or dismantle it, and nothing in between. That January he managed to evict Fucito from the premises, while commercial director Rimini decided to leave of his own accord. Fierce battles were fought, but at the end of six months of Gallo rule only one member of the Old Guard remained: Romeo. His massive stock holdings made his eviction difficult in the extreme.

On November 6, 1926 the Government created a powerful new entity called the Liquidations Institute (IL). It took over the BNC's functions and marked the transition from the private management of La Romeo to outright management by the State. It promised to be of the utmost utility to Gallo in his task. But only a few days later the fighting managing director became involved in a highly comprom-

Below left: The tragedy in which Ascari lost his life at the French Grand Prix at Montlhéry.

Romeo (just to the left of the top of the stairs) with members of his technical staff, 1925; Romeo's driving license.

ising political situation and, being a political Liberal in a Fascist regime, it also compromised his future with the State-controlled company. It took until September of 1927 to accomplish *his* eviction from the firm. But at the end of the year the IL found a means of resolving the case of Romeo by persuading him to give up his shares in La Romeo in exchange for the exoneration of debts which he owed elsewhere. The formal and final breaking of the ties between Romeo and the company which he had founded became official at the Board meeting of May 28, 1928, although his fate had been sealed at the end of 1925.

MOD. 21 F. T. A.
CIRCOLAZIONE DEGLI AUTOVEICOLI
(R. D. 31 dicembre 1923, N. 3043)
DUPLIC
Patente di abilitazione
di I.° GRADO
Firma del titolare
Nome, cognome e paternità Ing. Nicola Romeo di Maurizio
Data e luogo di nascita 28.4.1876 S. Antimo Provincia Napoli
Residenza abituale Milano
AVVERTENZA
Questa patente deve essere portata sempre sull'autoveicolo per esibirla ad ogni richiesta di funzionari e di agenti (art. 26 e 83)

Only a few weeks before that day of reckoning and almost half a year after his demotion to president, Romeo had gone to Paris to accept his appointment to Officer's status in the French Legion d'Honneur. Before checking into his hotel he drove to the circuit at Montlhéry, where he placed a wreath of red roses on the small granite stone which marked where Alfa driver Antonio Ascari had lost his life at the wheel of a P2 that July. While in Paris, Romeo granted a long interview to Charles Faroux, distinguished editor of the then very important daily newspaper, *l'Auto*. The result, which appeared in the issue of December 7, was Romeo's own story of his climb to success. He spoke as though he owned La Romeo lock, stock and barrel. He spoke of "when I bought Alfa," of "my factory at Saronno," and of how *he* continued to build railway cars in Naples and tram cars in Rome.

Asked by Faroux what he planned to undertake next, Romeo replied, "Now aviation concerns me a great deal. I want to take an important place in the field of aeronautical manufacturing. The base of Lucrino, near Naples, is going

"The first one to come to me about leaving Fiat was Ferrari," Jano told me in 1964. "But he was not in final authority and I was not happy about leaving Turin. I did not leave until Romeo sent his vice president to me."

Alfa's VP was Ing. Fucito and, according to Jano, it was the VP who, with his authority, really put the deal together. This did not jibe very well with Enzo's memoirs, in which he had said, "We discussed, I convinced him, he signed the next day." By way of comment on Jano's story, Ferrari wrote:

"He who did a little of everything at Alfa was the young engineer Rimini, who enjoyed the confidence of Ing. Romeo, a Catanian whose father was a director of the then famous Magazzini Mele, of Naples.

"Rimini, as commercial director, did everything. Alfa Romeo policy in racing was his handiwork. He held me in

The factory at Portello, in use for aviation engines, during or just after World War One.

Right: Monza, October 19, 1924. Rimini is second from right, in coveralls and armband. The scene includes many of the men with whom he worked in building Alfa's racing reputation: Jano (far left) and Luigi Bazzi (second from left). Front row, starting at cockpit: Giuseppe Campari, Antonio Ascari, Louis Wagner, Count Mario Carrobio, Nicola Romeo, and Rimini. Below: A 20-30 ES in the Targa Florio.

a certain consideration, evidently thinking that I could be useful to him. I had a car and went to Turin often and he gave me *carte blanche*: 'Ferrari, where there are competent people, carry them off by all tolerably legal means. . . .' ''

It was Rimini, not Romeo, who gave Ferrari the specific assignment to find a good man for the design department. Enzo, who also takes credit for having snatched engine specialist Luigi Bazzi from Fiat about three months before Jano, continues:

''When Bazzi and Jano came, only I and Rimini knew who they were, and what they were worth. Not Romeo, not Ing. Fucito, the vice president, nor Ing. Gradi, the plant manager. It was Rimini who, in person, lived that whole period, from the victory at Lyon in 1924 to the tragic death of Ascari the following year at Montlhéry, until the success in the Championship of Europe and of the World. Then, at a certain moment, Alfa Romeo quit racing and Ing. Rimini disappeared from the sporting scene. No one has ever known the reasons for the departure of Rimini from Alfa. It certainly must be linked to the changes at the top of the company. . . .''

Rimini left La Romeo in early 1926 as part of the exodus which was precipitated by the collapse of the founder's reign and the assumption of control by Pasquale Gallo, along with his sweeping reforms. It was a time of change and turbulence at Portello. Romeo's executive team, all loyal men of the south and including Rimini, left—almost to the last man. Other valuable men chose to leave the company at the same time, including Merosi and Jano's assistant, Molino.

Ferrari records that Rimini became director of a small motorcycle manufacturer named Gallino, after which he

Left: Exuberant fans after the 1924 GP victory at Lyon. Below: Ascari in the GP at Lyon. Bottom: The Alfa squadron at Lyon, 1924.

became sales manager of Magneti Marelli, a most important firm today. The two men remained in casual contact for several years.

In an article by Fusi on Nicola Romeo, published in the house magazine *Alfa Notzie* (January 1966) there is a photo of Romeo, Gradi, and a very young Rimini, said to date from before 1915. If this is correct, Rimini would appear to have been a part of the Romeo organization even before its absorption of Alfa. In 1985 Giulio Ramponi confirmed to me that Rimini had been Romeo's right-hand man and that Romeo had put him in charge of automotive sales. Racing is a fundamental tool of sales promotion and one can speculate that it was Rimini who persuaded Romeo to revive the active racing policy of Alfa before the war. Product philosophy generally would have to reflect this commitment to superior performance. It was a small company, with small output, and would give the sales/commercial director plenty of time to do a little bit of everything including product planning. Rimini's counsel as to what would win and what would sell was probably depended upon by Romeo and the Board. It was probably Rimini who first backed the RL program. He personally built up the staff of designers and technicians that he wanted. It was he who put out feelers for men like Bazzi and Jano and the sort of results that they could deliver, and he had the satisfaction of seeing many of his plans succeed. It was probably he who sold Romeo and the Board on the P2 project and on the 6C 1500, which was begun in the autumn of 1924. If it was not Rimini who guided product policy between 1920 and '25, we have no other clues as to whom it might have been. Romeo Rimini was the gorgeous name of one of his sons. The ultimate in euphemy.

UGO OJETTI

This very remarkable individual, one of Italy's leading citizens in his day, married Fernanda Gobba in 1905. Part of her inheritance when her father died in 1911 was his share in Nicola Romeo's then-small business. Ugo Ojetti took a most active interest in the management of his wife's fortune, which was a rare stroke of luck for Romeo, who thus found himself allied with a man in a million. At Romeo's invitation, Ojetti began to play an increasingly important but always discreet part in the company's affairs shortly after its acquisition of Alfa and its emergence as a big munitions manufacturer. When La Romeo became a public corporation in 1918 Ojetti was the heaven-sent choice for president, a position which he held until the BNC takeover and Romeo's hollow succession to the title. It was a sort of bonus that Fernanda Ojetti was the company's largest private stockholder.

Ugo Ojetti's greatest contribution to Alfa Romeo history consists in his diaries and, since his work kept him constantly on the move, his correspondence with his wife. These abundant, detailed records are packed with perceptive behind-the-scenes observations on what really went on inside and around La Romeo, and Prof. Bigazzi has made an exhaustive study of them, as with the rest of the literature pertinent to this period of Alfa Romeo's industrial history.

We learn from him that Ojetti was born in Rome in 1871, the son of a famous architect. He was a graduate in law, but soon turned to specialize in literature and journalism of the most erudite sort. In 1898 he began an almost 50-year career with Italy's great newspaper, *Corriere della Sera*, of which he eventually became managing director. He was a successful novelist and a leading critic of litera-

Below: Baldoni and Nasi in the 7th Targa Florio.

behind the leader, Guido Mergalli on a Nazzaro. The 22 year-old Ferrari then poured his all into making up for lost time, gaining four minutes and scoring the official fastest lap of the car-killing trial. Still, he could ''only'' finish 2nd and, in his own words, wept ''*come un bambino*'' when he learned the truth. Some journalists noted that, with better teamwork in the pits he might well have won. The press in general saluted an outstanding new talent of the first rank, while the brass in Milan felt its racing muscle harden.

It had been a lousy contest, with only 17 entries and mostly mediocre cars and drivers, only seven of whom were able to slog to the end. The only foreign entry was a less than fearsome Buick, which joined the national dropouts. Nevertheless, the Sicilian marathon was a classic race, and it brought overnight fame to the Alps and beyond to the nonentity from Modena. It catapulted Ferrari to the top-driver level in a flash, and it would forever remain one of the two most prestigious performances in his 12-year career of dicing with the speed kings. It was a fantastic start, the ultimate outcome of which was beyond anyone's imagination. Except Enzo's perhaps, in his wildest dreams.

Before the end of November Rimini had his driving crew signed up for the 1921 season. Campari remained the star of the outfit, joined by Ascari, Sivocci, and Ferrari. Franchini took up the less strenuous life of being ''merely'' a test driver and was replaced by a passing adventurer named Giuseppe Baldoni. The first gallop of this sturdy team was the Parma-Poggio, on May 8. Campari charged with the old GP car into a most honorable 2nd place. Baldoni seems to have stayed in reserve as the rest manned new Tipo 20/30 Sports. Engine trouble eliminated Enzo, as Ascari and Sivocci collected 1st and 2nd honors in their class.

Everyone had had enough of Sicilian winters, and for 1921 Vincenzo Florio staged his race on May 29, in radiant springtime. The change helped to attract 34 entries, including five Alfas. Four of them seem to have been ES's again, while Campari remained faithful to the old GP car, which was running extremely well. The team went in style this year, by train, instead of driving the racing cars from Milan to Naples and, if lucky, back again. Masetti's Fiat

The day after the 1920 Targa Florio, where Ferrari finished a remarkable 2nd overall. Left to right: Campari and Ramponi with the old 1914 GP car; Ferrari and Conti with a 40-60; Baldoni and Pieri in an ES 20-30.

won, Sailer's Mercedes was 2nd, and the name of Alfa Romeo filled the next three places out of the 19 finishers. Campari came in 3rd, while the allegedly stock ES chassis of Sivocci and Ferrari took the next honors. The marque was affirming itself with steadily increasing strength.

Next came the almost equally important circuit of Mugello, near Florence, on July 24. The top three finishers were Campari, Ferrari, and Sivocci — the finest performance in the history of Alfa to date. Enzo confirmed the class which he had shown in the Targa the year before.

August brought the 1433-mile Alpine Cup, an eight-day long series of dashing from one dizzying mountain pass to the next—from the mere 6168 feet of the Tonale to the 9042 feet of the Giogo dello Stelvio. It drew a fine 24-car field, out of which Sivocci and Enzo finished a respectable 4th and 5th, driving production ES Sports. A week later brought the Aosta—Gran San Bernardo, one of Europe's finest mountain races. Enzo took part with the current ES Sport, and again he finished 5th overall, winning his class. A young man named Pinin Farina, driving an Itala, was another touring-class winner, and it was on this occasion that the two men met for the first time.

Above: Ferrari's first victory came in 1923 at the Circuito del Savio. Right: The Alfa entries for the 1921 Targa Florio: (left to right): Sivocci, Ferrari and Campari.

In practice for the GP of Italy at Brescia in September Enzo rounded a curve on the supposedly clear course, only to collide with a few head of cattle. Miraculously, he and his mechanic walked away from the total wreckage of what had been a perfectly prepared 40/60 hp. In burning rage Enzo sought out the organizing officials whose negligence had cost a car and almost two lives. He was a powerful and eloquent young man and the violence of the dressing-down he gave them resulted in his permanent disqualification from competing in RACI (Royal Automobile Club of Italy) events. When passions had calmed, the Club's president made peace, and Enzo's outlaw status was rescinded. On that note, and obviously with a glorious future ahead of him, Ferrari ended his third season of racing.

For 1922 the first big race of the season, the Targa Florio, was eased back to an even more climatically ideal, April 2. It drew an enormous 45 entries, including a raft of foreign ones: Ballot, Bugatti, Austro-Daimler, Mercedes, Steyr, and Wanderer. Ascari, Sivocci, and Enzo were there, with alleged stock ES Sports. They finished 4th, 6th, and 16th. Enzo was well up with his teammates when he spotted Biagio Nazzaro's Fiat off the road and upside down, with both driver and mechanic pinned under it. To hell with the race. He stopped to free his comrades-in-arms, as they would have done for him. Sivocci threw his chances away to go to the rescue of Brilli Peri, who, with his mechanic, was trapped under his Steyr. Ascari's good 4th-place finish, against much swifter cars, underlined the price of being sporting and humane.

Top: Ferrari's ES Sport nears the finish line. Above: The victor leaves for home the day after the race.

Enzo was busy with other things in his complex life, and his only other race that year was the Aosta-Gran San Bernardo, in which he drove one of the Steyrs then being campaigned in Italy. He finished a dull 8th. We have no explanation for this switch of marques, the only one to interrupt his years with Alfa. The Italian agent for the Austrian make, Bruno Preserti, is said to have been a friend of Enzo's and this may have been a test to determine a business deal. Soon Preserti gave up Steyr and became the Alfa agent for all of Toscana.

Enzo did not race again until the Targa Florio in April

Right: Varzi in a P2 at the Targa Florio in 1930. Below: Ferrari, third from left, at Monza. Opposite top: Ferrari reaches out to congratulate Ascari, the winner at Monza in 1924. Opposite bottom: Ascari in a P2 at Montlhery in 1925.

1923, by which time big things had happened. Merosi's Tipo RL had been released in 1922 and the designer had now produced a lighter, more powerful racing version of the car, the RL TF. Plus, Rimini had recruited the talent of Count Giulio Masetti, who had won the Targa in 1920 (Fiat) and 1922 (Mercedes). The team for this year's race was therefore a formidable one, consisting of new competition cars driven by Ascari, Campari, Ferrari, Masetti, and Sivocci. The RL TF performed splendidly, on the whole, with Sivocci winning, Ascari coming in 2nd and Masetti 4th, out of an international field of 19 starters. Campari and Ferrari failed to finish. Enzo's problem was one of intra-team rivalry, which he later had the honesty to explain. He had decided to show Ascari how the Sicilian race should be driven, and he was indeed the faster of the two in practice. An inner voice warned him not to become over-confident, but he failed to pay it heed. In the race itself he finished the first lap ahead of the future champion and went charging on. He finally charged into a turn a shade beyond the limit, and wound up in a field.

only, he was lucky to hold onto 5th place until the end. It was an obscure happening in any case.

Not so the Mugello, which came a week later. It drew a terrific field. Campari, Nuvolari, Varzi, and Ferrari were all mounted on the cream of Alfa 1750's, and the rest of the best of the current vintage was there, including Hans Stuck and his Austro-Daimler. The day was a disaster for the Alfa works squad. The cars and/or drivers were in bad form, and Varzi's knowledge of the course was poor. The same Talbot-Darracq which had swept the field the year before did so again, this time driven by Brilli Peri. A 3-liter OM finished 2nd and an outsider, Enrico Benini, brought his Alfa home 3rd. Enzo loped in an inglorious 8th. His last race of the year was the Circuito delle Tre Province—80 miles from Bologna to Modena—which he failed to finish.

This quiet season was followed by a similar one for Ferrari in 1930. At Alessandria, on April 20, his 1750 GS finished a respectable 3rd, following Nuvolari in the updated P2 and Zanelli in a 2.3 Bugatti. In the Coppa Presolana, a very minor event near Bergamo on May 29, he was 3rd again, 12 minutes behind a private Alfa entry. In the Tre Province on August 10 Enzo did not finish, while the top two 1750 GS's were cars that he maintained. The 1st and 2nd-place finishers in the Coppa Acerbo a week later were Maseratis. Borzacchini's 1750 GS Alfa took 3rd spot while Enzo once again did not finish.

Enzo did not take the wheel in a speed contest again until June 14, 1931, and then the eight-mile hill climb near Piacenza was described as a reliability trial rather than as a race. He drove an 8C 2300 MM and permitted himself to be the first across the finish line. His last race was the Tre Province, on August 9. He drove flat out, in a marvelous dual for the lead with Nuvolari, who by then was one of the most brilliant drivers in the world. The lead changed many times, and when Nuvolari crossed the finish line in Modena he was only 32.8 seconds ahead of Enzo, who left this aspect of the sport in beauty. He later wrote, "I don't think that I behaved really badly as a racing driver."

OFF THE TRACK

What he had done was superb preparation for the fabulous career which was to follow. It is striking that his racing period is divided into two symmetrical, distinct, and radically different parts. The dividing line is like a wall between the Targa Florio of April 1923 and the Mugello of less than two months later. Before it, practically all of the events were first-class ones, of more or less national importance and of some international consequence as in the case of the Targa Florio. They were Big Time performances. After the boundary, Enzo involved himself almost exclusively in a whole different category of racing—small events of a strictly parochial character and greatly reduced risk.

It is interesting, appropriate, and logical that this line coincided with Enzo's marriage. He was 25, had had his fling at high adventure, and it was time to settle down. And then there was his business career to consider.

Ferrari has very little to say on this subject in his memoirs and it takes a great deal of research to piece together an idea of his business success, which is so intertwined with Alfa history. *My Terrible Joys* is by no stretch of the imagination an autobiography. It is a collection of scraps of information which the author desired to broadcast, and sorting the true from the less-true is no easy task. One of the images which Enzo wished to communicate was of himself as a self-made man who had risen from a squalid background. The climax of the latter comes in the winter of 1918-19, making him about 20 years old. After military service he is in miserable health and is freezing on a park bench in Turin, where Fiat has refused him a job. The picture is one of destitution.

But he does let it out that his father owned a metal-working establishment, of unspecified size and number of employees. And there was a "family car," which Enzo persuaded his father to teach him to drive in 1911, when he was 13. To own an automobile in the Italy of that day implies a socio-economic status that was well removed from squalor.

The 8C of 1935.

In *Terrible Joys* we read of Enzo's first race, in 1919. A remarkable find was pictured on page 9 of the Finarte (Modena) auction catalog for December 2, 1989. It is of the two sides of a postcard. One side shows Enzo, surrounded by a small crown of admirers. He is at the wheel of a large and splendid sports roadster—a Turin-built Caesar, rather like an American Crane Simplex of the World War I period. Enzo is wearing cap and goggles and is proprietarially relaxed. The contrast between these symbols of wealth and the squalid crowd is striking.

On the back of the card is written, in Enzo's hand, "Raid Pavullo-Sestola—July 19, 1917," referring to a competitive event held near Modena. It doesn't matter to whom the car belonged; the rank in the caste system is blatant. By the time he was freezing on a park bench a year and a half or so later, both his father and brother were dead. He did not speak of his mother, and may have inherited whatever constituted the family patrimony.

October 1920 found Ferrari somehow selected to drive on the Alfa team in the Targa Florio. Perhaps he bought the ride, as the well-to-do always have done. He was not aristocratic, though well-endowed with class. We know that he was accepted as a contestant in the Gran Premio Gentlemen at Brescia in 1921, meaning that he was accepted by the country-club set. In his memoirs he tells of having learned to read the fine print on a contract when he "bought" a car from Rimini. Fusi remembers that Tipo G1 and the incident. In his Merosi book he says that Enzo had Merosi modify the car to his personal specifications. That would have been in 1921, possibly '22; not long after the park-bench image. I am trying to form an image which fits those facts which are accessible to us.

On page 220 of the same Fusi book all the space is devoted to a most significant photo. It is of a close-up taken on the Alfa stand at the Salon de Paris in October 1923. It is the one photo I know of, of Enzo during his racing years, when he was wearing a business suit, an elegant one. He is as poised as a super-car-salesman as he ever was in mechanic's overalls. Innate class. Fusi's caption describes him as the distributor (concessionario di vendita) for the provinces of Emilia and Romagna (Marche would come soon after). By 1924 we have photos of Enzo not so much with the very top brass of the company as part of it — serenely at his ease with Romeo, Fucito, Rimini, and a few select others. The atmosphere is perfectly fraternal, as it might be among major stockholders. Enzo's letterheads were dominated by the Alfa emblem and, in large type, "Cav. Enzo Ferrari," followed by the addresses of his Modena and Bologna agencies and the title "Exclusive Sales Agent for EMILIA and ROMAGNA."

Valerio Moretti shares my feeling that when Ferrari returned to taking part in a few races, starting in 1927, an important part of his motivation was to sell cars, new and used. Enzo himself wrote, "I returned to racing for sporting enthusiasm and because of technical and commercial opportunities." As Giulio Schmidt points out, the success of the Mille Miglia race had fired public interest in sports and GT cars, which happened to be Enzo's stock in trade. The fact of his being allotted six-cylinder prototypes as rapidly as they appeared made clear the esteem in which he was held by the company in its very troubled times. Honesty, reliability, dynamism, organizational drive, and intelligence, among other assets, made him one of the company's most precious properties.

The consistent superiority of his racing performance must have had a depressing effect on sales to sportsmen who dreamed of an occasional win, which probably was related to Ferrari's backing off, starting in mid-'28. At the same time he was hatching a unique plan to sell cars and to race. It was the creation of a racing club or association which

Guidotti at the GP of Italy in 1937. He drove a 12C Alfa.

will be famous forever as the Scuderia Ferrari. The alterior motive was the typical one of stimulating racing, sales, and expert service and thus to generate cash flow. The S. A. Scuderia Ferrari was a corporation financed by well-to-do enthusiast stockholders and was constituted on September 1, 1929, just before the start of the Tre Province race, from which the managing director dropped out, letting his clients finish 3rd, 5th, and 6th.

The old Cav. Ferrari Alfa agency in Modena became club headquarters, providing the best of preparation and maintenance for its clients. It was much larger than the standard store front photos of the building suggest; its size was best appreciated from the air. Nor was the membership small. A photo of a typical club dinner in 1930 shows about 60 well-heeled members having a wonderful time, and there were others beyond the range of the camera.

Between its creation and dissolution in 1937 it was one of the most active one-make racing organizations in the world; perhaps the most. The splendid book by Orsini and Zagari, *La Scuderia Ferrari* (Florence, 1979), devotes 26 pages to its Alfa racing record, not to mention the Rudge and Norton bikes that Enzo raced between 1932 and '34. In the early years of the Scuderia it also served as an agency for Ford cars and Fordson tractors—also good for cash flow.

Because of hard times and the touchiness of racing with government property, Alfa and the IRI found it politic to use the Scuderia as an unofficial racing department. In 1933 the whole divine team of P3 racing cars was turned over to the Scuderia for campaigning. It became less of a club for wealthy amateurs and increasingly an effective factory branch, where cars were first maintained, then modified, then even designed and built wholly or in part by and at the Scuderia, on the factory's behalf and with its participation.

Enzo became the master-mind of the entire racing operation, except for design. He became a new sort of talent scout, first for the enlistment of established good drivers

Top: Ferrari, Nuvolari, Arcangeli and Siena during a race in the Thirties. Above: The Alfa Corse physical plant.

Enzo Ferrari at the age of 80.

and then for the creation of new good drivers. He made it his business to cultivate every possible string-pulling contact and he became, in his words, an agitator of men. He created a court at Modena, a center of growing power in the motor-racing world. Then, as described in the chapter on Ugo Gobbato, racing headquarters were moved back to Il Portello, Enzo with them, in 1938. Rather than settle for a future as a Milanese Neubauer, he behaved so outrageously as to get himself fired and handsomely indemnified the following year. He returned to Modena and his very special part of Italy with, as professional baggage, almost two decades spent at the vortex of the racing activity of one of the world's few really great marques in the competition field.

After World War II, when Enzo undertook to build his own competition cars and, soon enough, GT cars derived from them. He functioned as an Alfa Romeo alumnus might be expected to do. He began by hiring Alfa designer Colombo, then put another, Giuseppe Busso, in his place. His right arm was Luigi Bazzi, as much a product of the Alfa school as himself. He liked to attribute his choice of the V-12 engine configuration to Packards of the World War I era, but among the last cars he worked with at Alfa were Jano V-12s. He picked up where he had left off. Jano himself rejoined Enzo and Bazzi in 1956, as a still very sage consultant. Enzo worked and fought like a Titan, eventually making a considerable amount of money. But he needed help in many ways, the most urgent being with the management of an industrial organization which had outgrown his powers of control. And a looming necessity was that of providing for the survival of his creation after he should cease to be. And so it was he who, in 1966, requested of Fiat that it lend him Ing. Pierugo Gobbato to serve as La Ferrari's managing director. Pierugo was the son of the great Ugo. He had driven Scuderia cars in the early Thirties, and his relations with Enzo had always been good. Fiat granted the request, which led in a straight line to the famous accord of Ferrari with Fiat, the alma mater of so many of the actors in this epic and the parent company of Ferrari today, as it also is of Alfa Romeo.

Above: Bonetto, Ferrari, Giberti and Villoresi in 1949; right: Bonetto, Ferrari and Bignami in 1949. Opposite: Ferrari's last victory as a driver, at Bobbio-Passo del Penice in 1931.

Working for Alfa was unlike working for any other company in the world. It was a cult-like experience that penetrated many men's souls. Not all of its men fell under its spell, but for those who became true Alfisti—self-consciously elite of machine culture—it was something like initiation into a secret society. Once one had become an adept there was no turning back, even in rage. Ferrari was a quintessential Alfista and no doubt remained that until the day of his death. He remembered his first victory over the Tipo 159 Alfetta in 1951 thus:

"I wept with joy, but mixed with the tears of happiness there were also tears of sorrow, because on that day I thought: 'I have killed my mother.' "

This drew Oedipal pleasantries from observers who were insensitive to the meaning which this event held for the arch-Alfista who wrote the words. His poetic chords were touched again when he received a congratulatory telegram on the occasion of his marque winning its first World Championship in 1952. It had come from Alfa's managing director, but he replied to the whole confraternity:

> August 1952
> Dear Friends of Alfa,
>
> Allow me to thus begin this letter which I write to you after so many years.
>
> Your today's telegram has brought me a great flood of springtime and in the clear sky I have read, with striking clarity, the entire book of our memories.
>
> Twenty years I lived with you; how many facts, events, men have passed! Each and all I have recalled today.
>
> I still have for our Alfa, be certain, the adolescent tenderness of the first love, the immaculate affection for the mamma!
>
> Believe me.
> Your
> Enzo Ferrari

CHAPTER 5

VITTORIO JANO

Vittorio Jano
1891-1965
Design Engineer

IN THE CHAPTER ON GIORGIO RIMINI we have seen Ferrari's testimony concerning Rimini's role as instigator of talent raids on other firms, notably Fiat. It was he who pulled the strings which brought Vittorio Jano to Alfa and he who steered the racing program of the marque toward the road racing World Championship of 1925.

One day, Enzo goes on, Rimini asked him if he knew of a good man for the engineering department, of which Merosi of course was the head. Enzo questioned Luigi Bazzi, who had come to Alfa from Fiat. Bazzi told him: "There is a man of great worth at Fiat, who is being treated a bit as a subordinate. Go talk to him." Thus the contact was made. Enzo continues:

> "When Bazzi and when Jano came to Alfa Romeo, no one knew who they might be or what they might be worth. I knew it, and Rimini knew it. Not Romeo, nor Ing. Fucito, the vice president, nor Ing. Gradi, the plant manager. It was Rimini who personally was on top of that whole period, from the victory at Lyon in 1924 to the tragic death of Ascari the following year at Montlhéry, until the winning of the championship of Europe and of the world."

The instrument of and key to that phenomenal success was Jano's P2 GP car.

Jano was born in Turin on April 22, 1891. He was thirty-three years old when he came to Alfa; Merosi was then fifty-one. Jano's father was the technical head of one of Turin's two arsenals and it was traditional in the family that its men work in the mechanical and engineering arts. Jano told me how he had been born with a passion for machinery and engines and how, at age eighteen, he completed his technical studies at the Istituto Professionale Operaio di Torino. That was in 1909, and he promptly went

Bugatti 1.0 Atm, Fiat 1.3, Mercedes 1.4, Sunbeam 1.47, Alfa Romeo 1.7.

A real Achilles' heel of the Fiats was their valve springs, as it was for most high-performance engines until after World War II. The problem was that the available alloys would crystallize rapidly under high-speed use and, Jano said, Fiat would finish a race with ten or twenty valve springs broken. Those engines used three concentric springs per valve, for a total of forty-eight. Jano confronted this problem by using the same number of springs, but by making them fatter, higher and of larger-section wire—maintaining the same flexibility, as he put it, but with lighter spring loading. He was able to turn 6500 rpm with great reliability, as opposed to the Fiat's 5500 rpm, at which speed its valve springs would begin to collapse. Jano claimed in 1964 that with no other change than the adoption of modern improvements, such as have been made in valve springs and fuels, the P2 engine would be able to turn 8000 or 9000 rpm with ease. As it was in 1924, its 140 horses

were more reliable, if not stronger, than the 146 claimed for the Fiat 405. The P2's frame and running gear were essentially traditional although, as with the engine, Jano's ideas and touch were reflected in every part. The P2's showed up at Lyon for the GP de l'ACF in 1924 as dark horse entries, to whom hardly anyone gave a serious second thought. Besides Alfa and Fiat, Bugatti, Delage, Miller, Schmidt and Sunbeam were there, to make this one of the most telling and memorable Grands Prix of all time.

Originally, four P2 race cars were to compete in the grand prix and the chosen drivers were Giuseppe Campari, Antonio Ascari, Louis Wagner and Enzo Ferrari. Ferrari's car, however, did not muster the practice runs. After seven hours of hot, hard and extremely exciting racing, Campari led two Delages across the finish line.

The P2's walked away with it, not merely beating the supreme Fiats, but putting an end to that giant's long record of top-fight activity in racing. "That," Jano said, "was Alfa Romeo's birth announcement on the level of the *grandes épreuves*." And it marked the emergence of the marque as one of history's few great specialists in thoroughbred high-performance cars.

THE 6C 1500 SERIES

Alfa's management immediately began to study the sort of passenger car with which to replace the Merosi line. Jano had sounded the note with his P2 and what followed should be in harmony with it. The new generation of Alfa Romeo cars would emphasize brilliance of performance, along with outstanding roadholding, handling and braking. The rationale was given that since the norm for economy cars was four cylinders and one liter, while that of the middle level of the market was six cylinders and two liters, Alfa chose to set its sights on the market between these two: six cylinders and 1500 cc. The upcoming 1500 cc formula for GP racing may have been a factor in this decision. But, as things worked out, management decided to abstain from the Big Time for a spell and to base its racing activity on participation in sports-car events by enthusiast clients and a modest works team.

Opposite page, above: The Alfa garages at the GP d'Italia, 1924. Lower: Three views of the P2, one in Jano's own shorthand notation. This page: Campari in the moments following his victory at the GP at Lyon, 1924. The trophy lying across the hood is a giant salami, a specialty of Lyon.

1924 P2 race car, owned by the Alfa Romeo Museo.

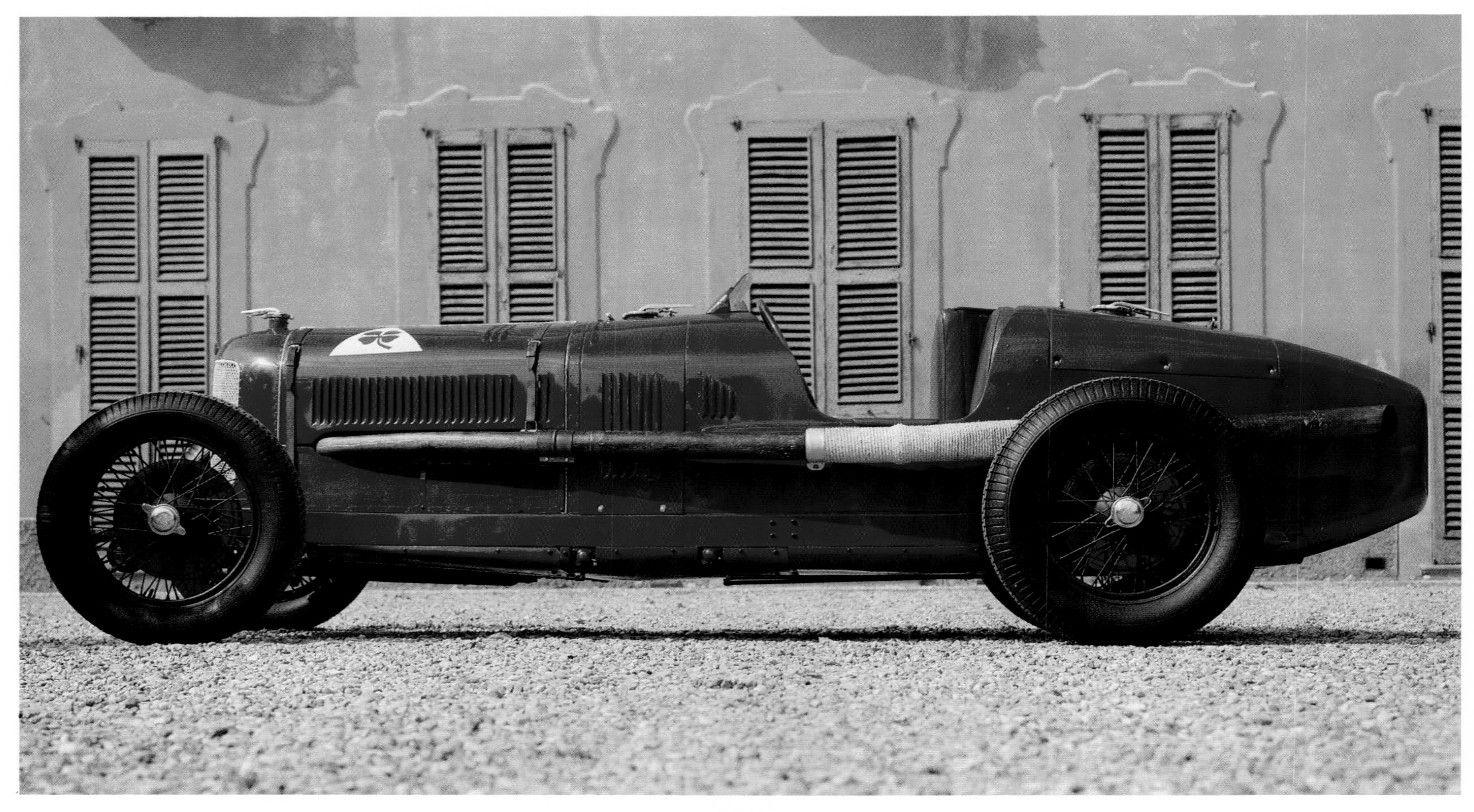

The die was cast in the fall of 1924, and Jano went to work on what has been termed "the archetype of the light and powerful modern Italian car." A prototype chassis made its bow at the Salone di Milano in April 1925 and then at the Paris and London shows. Five experimental long chassis and one short one were built in 1926, with production, sales and racing all beginning the following year. Aside from its worm-and-wheel steering and four-wheel brakes the new car, at first called the Tipo RN, had no particular points of similarity with the P2, nor with Fiat practice. It marked the beginning of Jano's long career of highly productive autonomy.

It was in this atmosphere of transition that the more traditionally oriented Merosi took his leave of Alfa Romeo. According to eye-witness Ramponi, those who have said that there was friction between Merosi and Jano are wrong.

1927 1500 Sport, body by James Young, owned by the Alfa Romeo Museo.

The two worked together in perfect harmony on the firm's 1924 Targa Florio effort, and on the revision of the RL. They respected each other and were great friends. While they represented radically different schools of design, they approached their work in much the same way. For example, both believed in thorough and lengthy road testing of any innovation. In terms of seriousness, meticulousness and patience, both had the same mentality. And, Ramponi stressed, "Their ideas were their own. I never saw in the drawing office a magazine that might have come from America, open to an article on Oldsmobile or something. Merosi enjoyed the competent, unsung support of Santoni, Jano enjoyed that of Luigi Fusi, Gioachino Colombo and Secondo Molino. It was young Molino who laid out the 6C 1500 before taking a better job at Bianchi." Jano told me that, from '33 on, he devoted only a small part of his time

A race between a Caproni 100 airplane, using a 6C 1750 engine, and an Alfa Romeo 8C 2300, driven by Tazio Nuvolari. The race was staged in Rome December 8, 1931, over a flying mile. The Alfa car won.

to racing, most of the work being done by "Colombo, who had become my right arm."

To return to the 1500, the car's chassis was conventional, with semi-elliptics all around, and torque-tube drive. The engine was a five plain-main-bearing six, with light alloy crankcase and deeply finned wet sump; the block and detachable head were of cast iron. The valves formed a single file down the center line of the head and were operated by an overhead camshaft with a four-blade cast aluminum fan at its front and shaft and bevel drive at its rear. A single updraft carburetor fed inlet manifolding which was cast inside the block of this clean and efficient-appearing engine. Ignition was by battery, coil and a 45-degree inclined distributor which was driven off the vertical camshaft drive. One element that was a radical innovation was the front axle, through which the front half-elliptic springs passed. Jano explained that the reason for this difficult and costly solution was the lowering of the car, whereas to make it underslung, with the springs passing under the axle, would have left it with insufficient ground clearance for the roads of the time. He categorically insisted that this was the first time that this system was used. He claimed precedence over Bugatti with the system, ignoring his own debt to Ing. Coda's earlier, series-produced Diattos.

The most original feature here was cam follower design, which Jano frankly acknowledged having derived from Hispano-Suiza practice. The classical Hispano follower is a mushroom type with two adjustable discs, the stems of which thread *into* the valve stem. The fact that this necessitates a very thick valve stem and therefore a heavy valve is relatively unimportant in large, slow-revving engines but out of the question in the opposite type. Wanting this sort of direct action of cam lobe on valve, Jano got around the problem, as well as the patent in question, by threading his discs *around* the valve stem. This elegant, light and highly efficient system would characterize all Alfa engines, touring as well as racing, until the changeover to cup or piston-type followers for the Giulietta Sprint in 1954. They happened to be hell to fabricate. The mildly tuned RN - perhaps standing for Tipo Romeo *Normale* - entered the world with a specific output of 30 bhp/L, which topped any *sports* model that Merosi ever had designed. (His RL SS delivered 24 bhp/L.) The RN's weight-to-power ratio was of the same order of superiority, and its performance was exciting.

Series production began in 1927, with 356 122-inch wheelbase chassis, called the 6C 1500 *Sei posti* (six passenger) or *Lungo*. It was looked upon not as a sports car, but as a light *gran turismo*. In the course of that year six 114-inch wheelbase chassis were produced, called the *Quattro posti* (four passenger) or *Corto*. They were the prototypes of the *Sport* or S models to come. These 1st Series *Lungo* and *Corto* models were continued into 1928, with production of 150 and 50 units respectively. The short-chassis cars, especially nervous and nimble, were raced by the enthusiast clientele with great brio and success.

Early in 1928 the 2nd Series of the 6C 1500 began, with the dropping of the old nomenclature, the long chassis becoming the *Normale*, or N, and the short chassis the *Sport*. The latter was transformed in character and prowess by the replacement of the sohc head with a beautiful twin-cam head which increased power output by about twenty-three percent. One hundred fifty-seven of these dream machines were built that year.

In the Mille Miglia that March, Campari drove an experimental blown version of the S, winning the race outright, while the first seven places in class were taken by unsupercharged sister cars. Campari's performance demonstrated the practicability of the supercharged small engine for fast touring purposes as well as for racing. Added to the line in 1928 was a high-compression version of the S, called the SS, and added to the SS was a supercharged production version. Development of the 1500 culminated, still in feverish 1928, with the production of a handful of supercharged *testa fissa* (fixed- or integral-head) models for the use of the house team. They pulled 84 bhp/L. Thanks to the 6C 1500, the team and the hard-charging clients, Alfa Romeo became, on Italian road and mountain courses, what it had been on GP circuits thanks to the P2. When production ceased in 1929, only 1058 6C's of all sorts had been built, each one a collection piece.

For 1929 the cylinder dimensions of the 6C were increased from 62 x 82 to 65 x 88 mm, giving birth to the 1750 line. It followed the same stages of development as had the 1500. The additional displacement was not utilized to increase power output, but rather to increase comfort through reduction of stress on engine, chassis and occupants. It is not true that the 1750 can be identified by its

The fire department of Aosta, Italy, outfitted with an Alfa Romeo 1750 roadster for the chief.

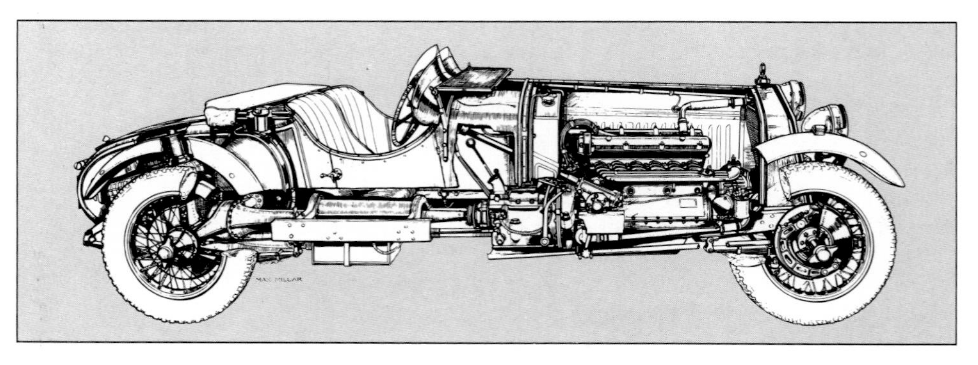

Above: A cutaway drawing of a 1929 Alfa Romeo 6C 1500 SS. Below: 1928 1500 SS, owned by Count Giovanni Lurani.

sloping radiator. The last specimens of the 1500 SS had them too, to make room for the supercharger, mounted low in front of the engine. Unblown 1750's had vertical radiators.

Although fundamentally an engine and chassis man, Jano had his own clear ideas about how his cars should be bodied and he consulted with the firm's principal coachbuilders on the appearance that he wanted his cars to have. According to Fusi, Zagato, with the single-cam sixes, was the first to express Jano's thoughts on body design. And it was Jano, he recalls, who suggested to Zagato the use of lightweight tubular body framing, in place of the traditional wood.

Alfa phased out the 1750 in 1933, after building 2579 units, of which 714 were bare chassis and 1865 complete cars. In that last year, forty-four *Gran Sport* chassis were built, using lightening-holed welded box-section frames rather than traditional rails, and also a light-alloy cylinder head for the first time. A similar chassis, with piston displacement of 1917 cc, thanks to a bore of 68 mm, was called the 6C 1900 GT, of which 197 complete cars were made. This was another feature in the direction of passenger comfort, the unsupercharged engine providing the silence and fuel economy which the blown cars lacked, along with good flexibility and almost as spirited performance. This engine constitutes the genealogical bridge between the 6C 1750 and the 6C 2300 - a new level of touring comfort which was attained in 1935.

The next step in Alfa evolution was the development of the 8C 2300, begun in 1930 and introduced at the Mille Miglia in April 1931. It was a true *competition* sports car: one designed as a road racer which also could be built in small series and equipped for touring. Like that of the P2, the engine had ten main bearings, and it was very largely an eight-cylinder version of the 6C 1750, retaining the same

bore and stroke along with many other engine and chassis parts. But, for the first time the cylinder blocks (two) were light-alloy castings with dry steel liners, and the cylinder heads also were of light metal. Dry sump lubrication was used. A really breathtaking architectural elegance was achieved by Jano in the design of this engine by making the crankshaft in two parts, with two helical spur gears between them. One drove the Roots blower which nestled against the right side of the crankcase, the other a train of gears which drove the camshafts. This central drive of course helped to reduce to the vanishing point timing aberrations due to torsional windup of the camshafts. The same basic layout had been used in 1928 by French engineer Emile Petit for his 1100 cc straight-eight Salmson GP engine. Luigi Chinetti, who was with Alfa at the time, has told me categorically that Jano's inspiration for that aspect of the 2.3 liter eight and its successors was indeed the Petit eight. Jano later would use a separate blower for each block, also in the manner pioneered by Petit.

The 8C 2300 chassis was divine in appearance, in design, in performance and in handling. Only 207 8C 2300's were made before the end of the run in 1934. Bodied for the track and for the road, they richly enhanced the racing record and purebred image of the marque. Among very discriminating Bugattistes they often are preferred on all counts to Bugattis. In spite of all this, Jano remembered these splendors, including the 8C 2300 Monza monoposto, with repugnance. "That chassis was simply too heavy," he said. "It was no masterpiece of mine."

1931 1900 GTC, by Touring Superleggera, owned by Giulio Dubbini.

THE TIPO A & TIPO B

For the 1931 season Jano designed his and Alfa's first monoposto for formula racing. Had its power sources possessed a crankcase in common, the assembly would have been called a U-12. The power train consisted of a pair of 6C 1750 engines and gearboxes mounted side by side, each set up with outboard exhaust and inboard intake systems. Behind each transmission (their neatly inter-linked shift mechanisms did not compensate for their redundancy) was a drive shaft which delivered torque to its own ring gear, pinion, stub axle and rear wheel. The car was terribly potent but, dogged by problems, the best that Campari and Nuvolari could do with their Tipo A's was a first and third in the 188-mile Coppa Acerbo at Pescara in the Abruzzi that year. With another non-masterpiece to his credit, Jano went back to the drawing board.

From its victorious first appearance in the Italian GP at Monza in June 1932 the Tipo B was called the P3, in recognition of it being a worthy successor to the immortal P2. It was and is one of the great automobiles, racing or otherwise, of all time.

Its body was narrower but not too unlike that of the old

Above: Nuvolari fills the tank of his Alfa at the G.P. d'Italia, 1931. He and co-driver Campari won the race. The Jano era in Alfa technology. Clockwise from below left: Cross-section of the six-cylinder 1750 SS engine; Campari and Giulio Ramponi in a 1929 1750 SS; cross-section of the 8C 2300 engine; a 1931 8C 2300.

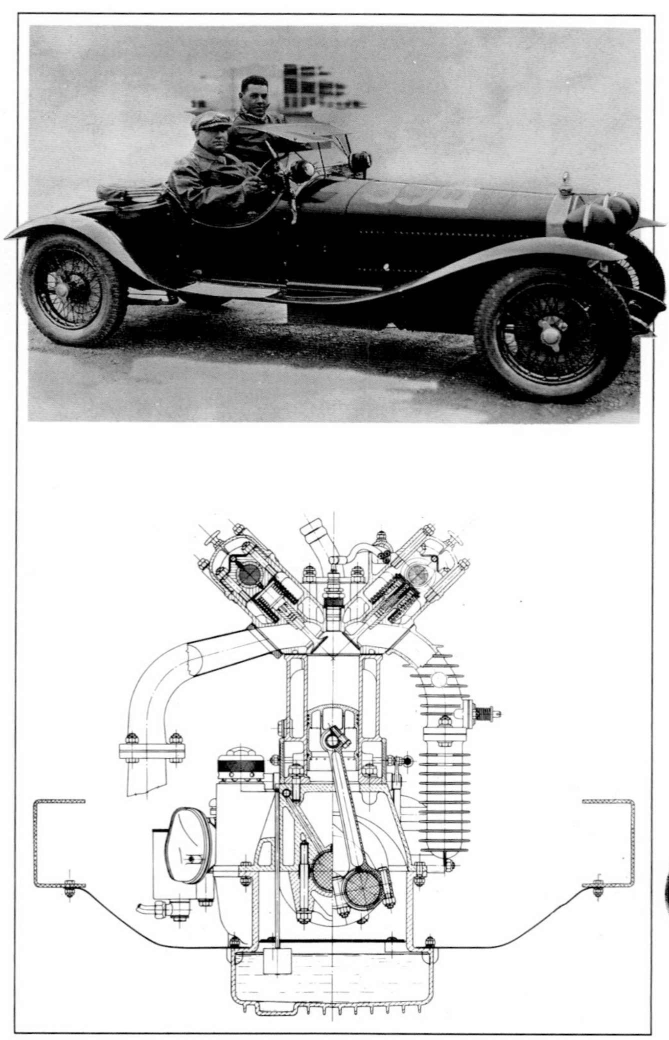

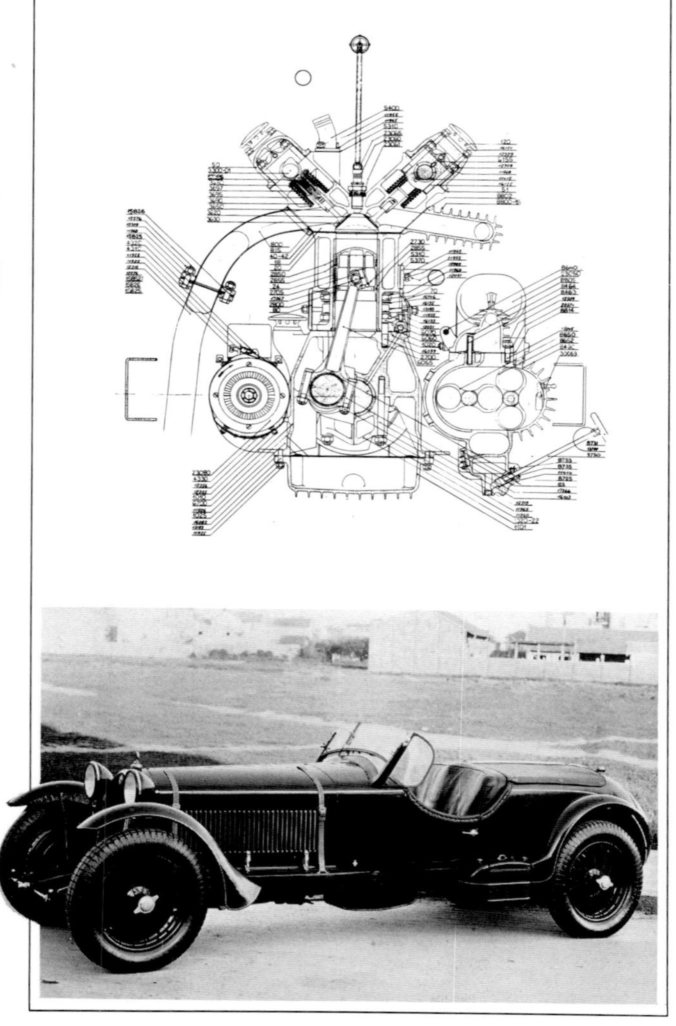

P2. The form of its radiator was reminiscent of that of the 3.0 liter straight-eight Ballots of 1920, which had been style-setters in other ways. Like the Type 59 Bugatti, it was a culmination of Twenties tradition. Up to a point, its chassis was conventional, with half-elliptics passing over the front axle and under the rear axle. But it incorporated a small differential housing just behind the transmission, from which branched two drive shafts which formed a "V" terminating in a pinion and ring gear at either side of a single live rear axle. The arrangement probably was a spin-off from the Tipo A, and its purpose was to allow the driver of this monoposto to sit far lower than would be possible with a central drive shaft. In practice it seemed to work as well as it did in theory. Brakes continued to be mechanically operated, and their drums filled the wheel rims. The frame kickup over the rear axle was by far the highest that Jano ever had used. The car was low, skinny, aerodynamically clean and totally classic. Nineteen thirty-two was a great vintage year, and the P3 helped to make it so.

Under its bonnet was one of the most beautiful engines, both inside and out, of all time. It can be described as an integral-head extrapolation from the 8C 2300, with ten plain main bearings but now with a separate Roots blower for

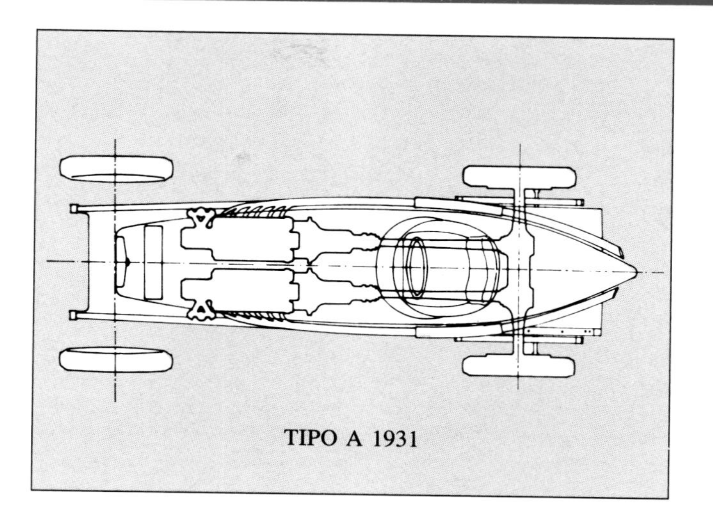

Below left: Cross-section of the Tipo B engine and an experimental "aerodynamic" Tipo B of 1934. Right: A planview of the 1931 Tipo A.

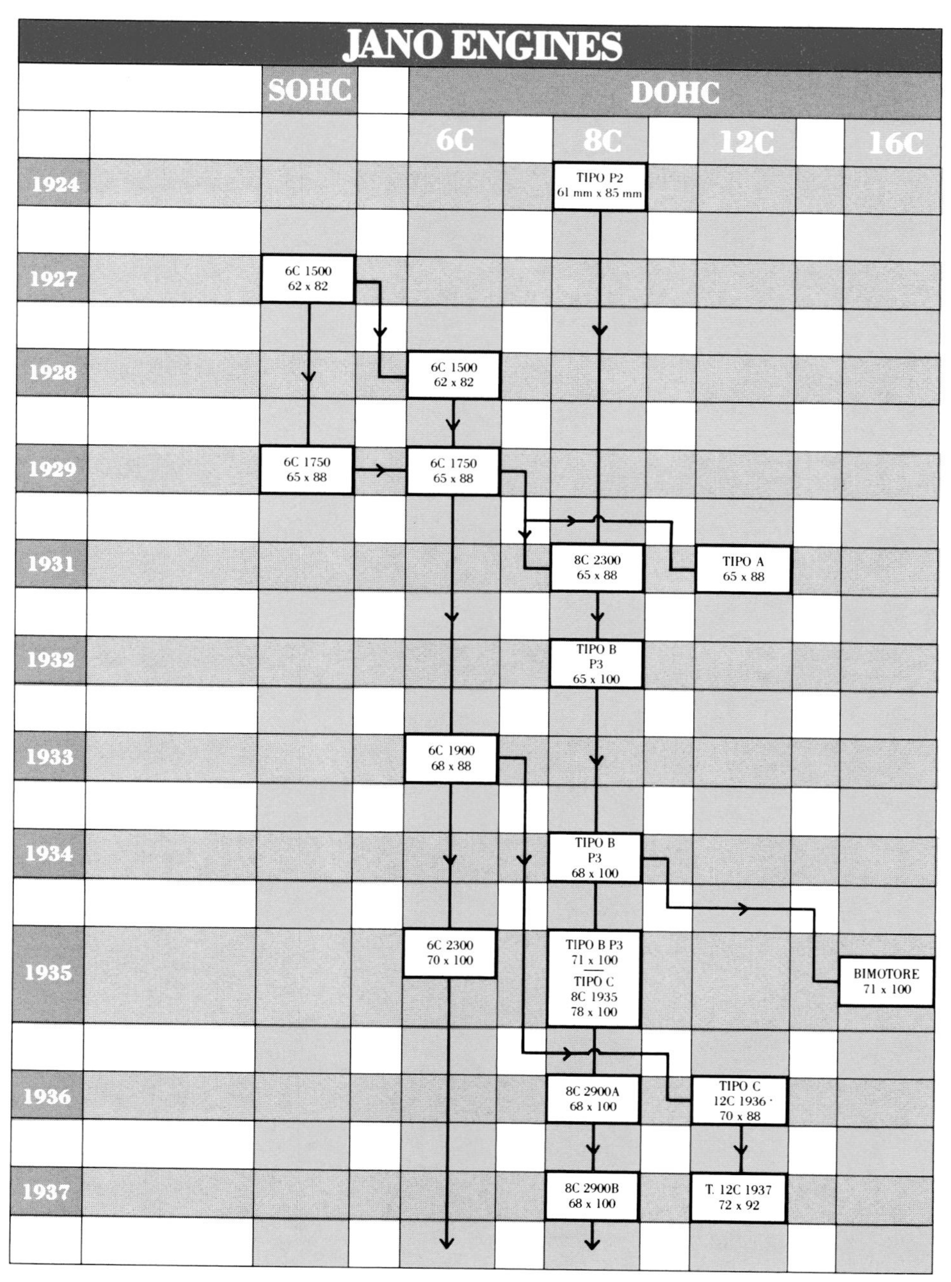

each block of four cylinders. The gear train, instead of being helical, was straight-cut. While the block-head castings still were of aluminum alloy, the crankcase and sump were of magnesium. One of Jano's chief objectives with this machine had been to break new ground in weight/power ratio, which he did. With the new engine putting out 215 bhp from its initial 2654 cc. the car weighed just nine pounds per hp, dry. Bore and stroke remained at 65 x 100 mm until the end of the 1933 season. In 1934 the bore was increased to 68 mm, displacement to 2905 cc, and output to 255 bhp. In '35 the bore was taken out to 71 mm, resulting in 3165 cc and 265 bhp, and two cars for the French GP had engines with 78 mm bore, giving 3822 cc and 330 bhp. The P3 amassed a beautiful competition record in

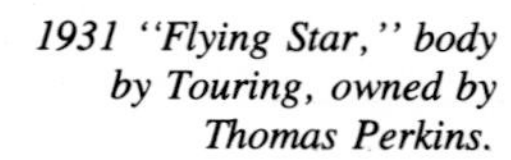

1931 "Flying Star," body by Touring, owned by Thomas Perkins.

1932 and '33, following which it became outclassed by its German rivals. It was a source of lifelong satisfaction to Jano who, near the end of his days, said, "That was a generous engine. It was perfect."

The Salone di Milano of April 1934 was marked by the introduction of a new Alfa line, which would replace the existing hierarchy of sixes and remain in production for long years to come. This new 6C 2300 chassis had a box-section frame similar to that which had been presented on the previous year's sixes. The flatness of its ride was enhanced by outboard mounting of its half-elliptic springs, which were anchored in rubber. Now the four-speed transmission boasted synchronization of the top two gears, along with free wheeling. This mixed blessing was controllable

1931 Tipo A (replica), owned by the Alfa Romeo Museo.

Right: The Alfa Romeo display at the 1932 Salone di Milano. The 8C 2300 that won the sixth Mille Miglia is displayed most prominently. Below: Jano with Rudi Carracciola, 1932.

from the instrument panel, as were the rear shock absorbers. The crankcase and block of the now seven main bearing engine consisted of a single casting, while the cylinder head was in light alloy, like those of the 6C 1900 and the 8C 2300. Gear drive to the overhead camshafts of his previous touring car engines had been chosen, Jano said, because chain drive had not been reliable beyond about 4000 rpm. That problem had been overcome, and the new engine's camshaft drive was by silent chain at the front. With the ample displacement of 2309 cc and use of a twin-throat updraft carburetor, the thrill and expensive luxury of supercharging could be dispensed with. Alfa's management had told Jano to tame his road machines and a new, civilized but still highstrung breed had been born. Purists lamented the passing of the machined-from-the-solid feel and the sacred sounds of yore.

The company established its own in house body-building facility in 1932-33, where most of its series-production bodies were made, although specialist coachbuilders continued to be used. A trio of the new sixes in high-performance, 95 bhp form and wearing identical Touring berlinetta bodies finished 1-2-3 in the 24 Hours of Pescara in 1934, giving birth to the Pescara top-of-line range in this series.

Lord Howe drives an 8C 2300 to victory in the 1931 Le Mans; his teammate was Tim Birkin.

1932 8C 2300 Mille Miglia, owned by the Alfa Romeo Museo.

1932 8C 2300 roadster, owned by Thomas Perkins.

Three 12-cylinder, four-liter Alfas at the GP de Monaco, April 13, 1936: Nuvolari leads the pack and eventually finished fourth; Farina, next in line, finished fifth, he is followed by Brivio.

Refined as it was, the 6C 2300 still was raceworthy, and thus worthy of the Alfa name.

While the racing department at Milan worked on a new V-12 monoposto, a different machine to challenge the thundering Germans was devised and built for the 1935 season at the Scuderia Ferrari in Modena, then virtually an Alfa factory branch. Even from that distance, there was much about the car that was pure Jano, such as its P3 engines and twin diagonal drive shafts, but in our conversations he ignored this offspring which was most notable for its brute strength. Its formal name was the *Monoposto Bimotore* of 1935, and good authority credits its design to Luigi Bazzi.

Unlike the Tipo A of 1931, which had side-by-side engines and thus more frontal area than anyone wanted, the *Bimotore* had one of its big, 3165 cc straight-eights in the normal position and the other longitudinally behind the driver and centered over a swing rear axle. With Dubonnet ifs, this was one of the first Alfas to have four-wheel independent suspension. The layout of the power train was elegant and dazzlingly ingenious. There was a single multi disc clutch at the rear of the front engine, and behind it a three-speed gearbox. Aft of it was a differential, and then the splayed, P3-type drive shafts. Then, the output shaft from the rear engine extended forward, *through* the differential and transmission to telescope through the tubular output shaft from the clutch and link up with the front engine's flywheel.

With an output of 540 bhp this was the most powerful Alfa thus far, carrying a record low four pounds per horsepower. Still, with a dry weight of 2266 pounds - 671 more than the current P3 - it was impossibly heavy and it was not an engineering solution to the winning of races. While its tires held together it was very fast, Nuvolari having been clocked in one of the two cars on the Firenze-Mare Autostrada in June 1935 at 226.30 mph. The sound of all those spur gears, ball races and four Roots blowers screaming at 5000 rpm-plus, must have been a trip, especially for the driver at the vortex of it all.

The design and development of a suitable replacement for the P3 Tipo B began in 1934, the first year of the 750 kg GP formula. Its bodywork was much more aerodynamically clean than that of the existing *monoposto*. Independent suspension all around was provided by a new Alfa coil-spring system at the front and swing axles at the rear, where the change-speed transmission formed a unit with the final-drive housing. Power was provided by the already mentioned 330 bhp, 3.8-liter P3 type engine. It was a fine try but, confronted by the daunting M25 Mercedes-Benz with 430 bhp, it was outclassed.

Alfa's first V-12, released in 1936, was exceptionally beautiful as a bare chassis. The engine's light-alloy cylinder blocks had the habitual integral heads and dry liners. Camshaft drive, by a train of spur gears, was at the rear of the engine, while a single large Roots blower was driven from the front of the crankshaft. The lower-end bearings were plain, as in all Jano engines since the P2, and the piston stroke happened to be that of the 1750 of fond memory. It may have been this art object of a power plant that tied the knot on Enzo Ferrari's love affair with the V-12 form.

The 70 x 88 mm, 4064 cc 12C developed 370 bhp at 5800 rpm. Its specific output of 91 bhp/L was the highest in Alfa history, and the car weighed only five pounds per horsepower. In 1936 it did very well, thanks to the driving of Tazio Nuvolari. He finished first in the Spanish GP, second in the Eiffelrennen, first in the Milan GP, second in the Italian GP, and first in the Vanderbilt Cup on Long Island that October, to the astonishment of American spectators. The *grandes épreuves* of 1937 were totally dominated by the Germans. In the GP of Italy the best Italian finisher—Nuvolari in a 1936 12C—could do no better than seventh. The cars achieved a fine racing record—in Italian national events, against national competition.

1932 Alfa Tipo B Grand Prix car, owned by Don Young.

Right: The Mille Miglia, 2900A. Below: The board at the mid-Thirties GP d'Italia displays the ascendency of the Germans and the fallen grace of the Alfas. Below right: Jano's answer, the supercharged V-12.

THE 8C 2900 SERIES

The 8C 2900 A, also begun in 1934, was, quite simply, a two-seat, sports-racing version of that year's P3 GP car, with engine detuned to supply 220 rather than 255 bhp. Weighing all of 1870 pounds dry, it had to pull a mere nine pounds per horsepower. It had the same all-around independent suspension as the Tipo C. The model made its debut in the Mille Miglia in April 1936, sweeping the first three places with ease. These were, essentially, open-wheel racing cars built for two, to which cycle fenders and headlights had been added. They were followed by similar chassis fitted with proper street bodies and then in 1937 and '38, by the 8C 2900 B,

Left: The 1936 12C. Below: Jano in his later years, at the wheel of a 1750 roadster.

detuned to 180 bhp for road use and fitted with dashing and luxurious coachwork by Touring and Pinin Farina. For the times, they cost a fortune, as did their engines alone. They stand as an ultimate among ultimate cars. Only twenty-six were made.

THE TIPO C - 12C 1937

This GP car was Jano's swan song at Alfa Romeo. Its chassis seems to have been basically that of the Tipo C, with extensive modifications to the engine. Bore and stroke were increased from 70 x 88 to 72 x 92 mm displacement from 4067 to 4495, and the plain con rod bearings were replaced with rollers. Jano substituted two smaller, much faster-turning blowers for the previous large, single unit and obtained an output of 430 hbp at 5800 rpm—very close to 100 bhp/L, and a new all-time record for the marque. The engine weighed only 473 pounds, and the car weighed only four pounds per horsepower, matching the *Bimotore* monster.

One of these cars was entered, already late in the season, in the Coppa Acerbo on August 15, but was not raceworthy. Five Alfas were entered in the Italian GP at Livorno a month later: a 1935 8C, three 1936 12C's and one new 1935 12C. That car broke a rear axle and the Germans roared into the first six places, the Alfas doing no better than 7th, 9th and 10th. According to Fusi, "the negative result in this race cost Jano his parting with Alfa Romeo."

The conditions underlying that break went back for years and were much more profound. One very likely element was that Jano was expected to design and build winning racing cars on a very restricted budget. Another was that, following Merosi's departure, he became the chief engineer, responsible for the entire technical sector at Alfa Romeo. Under the administration of Ugo Gobbato, in early 1934, he was reduced to the automotive sector alone. It produced only 699 touring and racing cars that year, 91 in 1935, 10 in 1936 and 270 in 1937. It was said that he was used up, "a squeezed lemon," and others began to move into his territory, starting with Colombo and Trevisan. Finally, in the last half of 1937, he and Gobbato had a heart-to-heart talk, and the great hero left the scene of his conquests. He achieved fine things in the future, but he did not achieve them essentially alone, as in the past.

1934 Tipo B Aerodynamica, owned by the Alfa Romeo Museo.

As Jano spoke to me of that parting, he explained that Vincenzo Lancia had died earlier that year. Lancia always had been the great source of technical leadership in his company and his loss was deeply felt. Needing help, the company made Jano a very attractive offer of the directorship of its experimental department, of what we would call R&D. He was forty-six, had been away from his native Turin for thirteen years, and would be glad to return to home, family and friends. At the end of the four years of warfare which had been the 750 kg Formula, Jano left the competition arena . . . for a while. He left behind a quite literally fabulous tradition, one that he had done more than any other man to create.

His stature as an automotive engineer was there to be recognized, and it dated, from his beginnings at Alfa Romeo. What has received surprisingly little recognition is his stature as an artist in metal. In his work, extraordinary function and form were inseparable aspects of the same total concept and feeling. His work was pointed at to "prove" the platitude that when form follows function, beauty results. In getting his ideas successfully down on paper, for realization in metal, he was fortunate in having the support of Luigi Fusi and Gioachino Colombo, engineering draftsman and designer respectively, whom he had begun forming when Fusi was seventeen and Colombo twenty-one. Colombo would carry the Jano/Alfa design tradition to brilliant new heights: the World GP Championship-winning Types 158 and 159.

1936 Tipo C, owned by the Alfa Romeo Museo.

CHAPTER 6

UGO GOBBATO

Ugo Gobbato
1888-1945
President

OUR CHAPTER on Giuseppe Merosi opens with the famous quotation by Henry Ford: "Every time I see an Alfa Romeo pass by, I lift my hat." It has been repeated countless times in Alfa company literature and perhaps as often in independent writings. I have asked company people for the source of this rather unlikely legend, but none of them has been able to reply with more than a shrug of the shoulders. A letter addressed to the Ford Archives in the United States brought this answer: "This has come up before, and we've never been able to verify it. It is implausible and apocryphal."

Imagine my surprise, then, when, in the middle of a long interview session with Dr. Ing. Pierugo Gobbato in 1988, he let drop this morsel:

"I remember that my father visited Henry Ford in Dearborn in 1939. That was when Mr. Ford said to him, 'When I see an Alfa Romeo, I lift my hat.' "

"So *that* is the origin of that story," I said, "How did Mr. Ford happen to say it?"

"Well, he asked my father, 'How many cars do you make per day?' My father, exaggerating a bit on the high side, said, 'Oh, about six.' And Mr. Ford laughed and said, 'I make that many in a minute.' "

"Aside from that, do you know how Mr. Ford came by any opinion at all about Alfa cars?" I asked. "Very few ever came to the States in those days."

"I seem to remember that in 1938, Mr. Ford had examined an 8C2900 roadster that had been bought by a member of the Rockefeller family. In any case, I know that he respected their design and workmanship."

"But '*tutte le volte*,' as one usually sees in print, makes it sound as though he saw Alfas fairly frequently."

"Mr. Ford has been misquoted. He didn't say, 'Every

1934 Alfa Romeo 2300GT coupe by Castagna, owned by the Alfa Romeo Museo.

time I see one.' He said, '*When* I see one.' My father recounted that episode to me, and the exact words are still clear in my mind."

In January of 1933, a new, more powerful and efficient State-owned entity, the IRI, took over the functions and responsibilities of the Istituto di Liquidazioni, including the ownership of Alfa Romeo. This same IRI is stronger than ever in Italy today. That autumn, looking for the man most ideally qualified to assume the firm's management, the IRI offered the position to Ing. Ugo Gobbato, one of the more distinguished management experts in the history of European industry.

Gobbato had returned that July from a two-year mission in Moscow. He was in such a state of physical and nervous exhaustion that he questioned whether he ever would be able to work as he had in the past. Job offers came to him immediately — big ones from both Fiat and Lancia — but he would not commit himself. Eventually, his strength and energy came back, and with them came the IRI offer of the

challenge of his dreams. He took over as managing director of Alfa Romeo on December 1, 1933, and began whipping the derelict company into a finely tuned industrial organization for the first time in its quarter-century of life. The other jobs would have been routine and easy, with little satisfaction at the end of the line. But if he could pull off the salvaging of Alfa Romeo, that achievement would be its own reward. And making the effort for his own government stirred his patriotic soul.

Ugo Gobbato was born on July 16, 1888, in an obscure spot, called Volpago del Montello, in the province of Treviso, slightly to the north of Venice. His parents were small landowning farmers. As a young teenager, Ugo studied for and obtained a "technical license" — a sort of diploma — in the city of Treviso, where he also worked in an electric generating plant. With some money saved, he moved on to Vicenza, took another job and also attended the Rossi Industrial Institute, where he earned his diploma as a *perito industriale* in electricity and mechanics. (P.I. is a title given by schools which are not accredited to give engineer's degrees). Then came another job and a move to Germany, to work as a draftsman and also attend the Zwickau School of Engineering. He received his Mechanical Engineering degree in March, 1909 and his Electrical Engineering degree that September, having recently turned 21.

Returning to Italy, young Ing. Gobbato performed his compulsory military service from December, 1909 to December, 1910, assigned to working with pioneer aircraft and radio. From 1912 through 1915, he was employed at the Marelli electrical factory, near Milan. He was in and out of the Army, always close to aircraft, until 1916, when he was activated for the duration of World War One. During the war, Gobbato was involved in the construction and development of the SCAF aircraft factory, in Florence. Except for his stint with Marelli, this was his first taste of industrial organization and the real start of his career.

Discharged from the Army in March, 1919, Gobbato immediately applied for a position with Fiat in Turin. After a review of his background, he was assigned to a study program devoted to reconversion of the company's automotive division to peacetime conditions. The firm had long since outgrown its original manufacturing facilities in Corso Dante and had overflowed into small feeder shops scattered throughout the local area. The crying need to house the entire operation under one roof had led Senator Giovanni Agnelli, then managing director of Fiat, to conceive the giant Lingotto factory in 1914. ("Senator" was an honorary title, which Nicola Romeo also received.) Construction was begun two years later, only to be delayed while war came and went.

The monolithic structure consisted — and still does — of two parallel blocks of reinforced concrete five stories high,

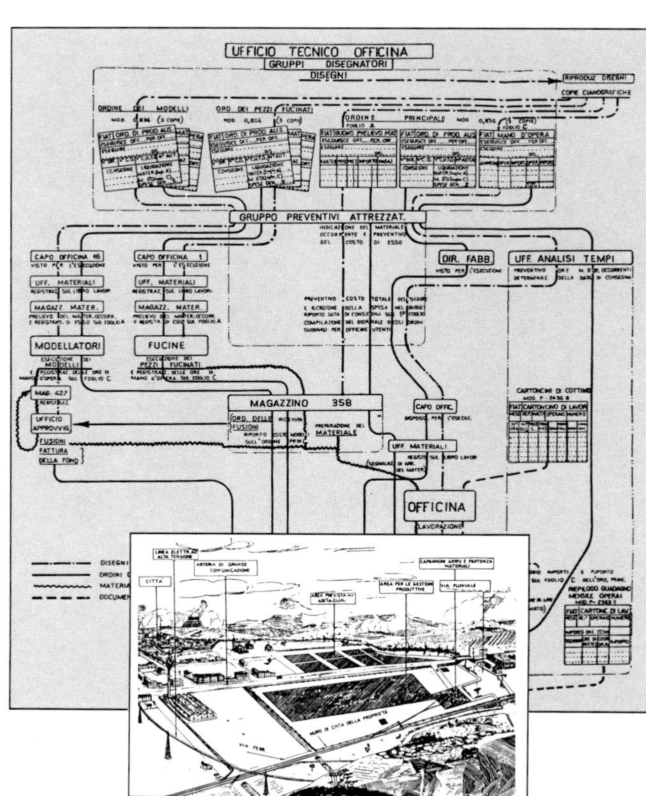

An excerpt from Gobbato's book, Organization of the Factors of Production.

Benito Mussolini in an Alfa Romeo 2300 parade car.

1,640 feet long and joined at either end by spiral ramps leading to a test track on the roof. Work on the world-famous edifice was completed in 1923. As Gobbato's talent revealed itself, he was soon put in charge of equipping the empty new building with machine tools and every other necessity for production, from the design stage, through component fabrication and assembly, to final testing. He was also made responsible for the integration at the Lingotto of all of the company's dispersed automotive production facilities. Reporting *directly* to Agnelli, who became president in 1920, technical director Fornaca, and administrative director Valetta, Gobbato completed the Herculean task in 1922. Having thus proved himself, he was assigned to manage the giant factory, which remained for years a model of modern industrial organization and production technique. Under Gobbato, its output reached 300 cars per day. In 1923, Benito Mussolini, head of the newly installed Fascist government, made a tour of inspection of the plant, guided by Gobbato. He was deeply impressed by all that he saw, including the 35-year-old plant manager.

Gobbato had a strong interest in education and, early on, he created an apprentice school and a night school for Fiat employees, present and future. As he became recognized as a leading expert in industrial organization, he began teaching courses on this subject at the Turin Polytechnic and at the city's Industrial Institute, picking up the title of professor along the way. His lectures formed the basis of the textbook, *Organization of the Factors of Production*, which he also illustrated. The first edition appeared in 1928 and the work remained in print until 1949. It begins with chapters on the selection of product and factory site, covers the whole industrial productive process, and closes with a section on industrial cost analysis.

In 1929, with Il Lingotto running smoothly, Fiat put Gobbato in charge of the reorganization and modernization of a recent acquisition, the NSU factory in Neckarsulm, Germany. On this mission, which took less than a year, he commuted to the job site from his home in Turin, where he continued to teach.

In 1930, Gobbato was sent to Spain, to oversee the organization of Fiat España, in collaboration with Hispano-Suiza, Pescara, and Ricart España. This was the beginning of his relationship with Wifredo Ricart, who rejoined him six years later at Alfa Romeo.

In about 1930, and in connection with its first five-year plan, the Soviet Union invited proposals from Germany, Italy, Sweden, and the United States for the construction

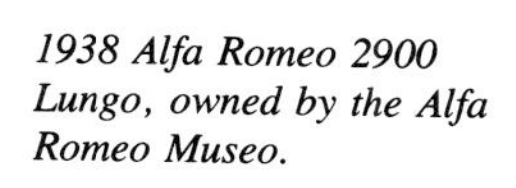

1938 Alfa Romeo 2900 Lungo, owned by the Alfa Romeo Museo.

Above: The central foundry at the Portello factory. Below: An allied aerial photo marking the Portello factory for bombing, 1944.

dismissal, so that he could return to Modena independent and well-heeled.

Following the failure of the V-12 racing car, Gobbato put Trevisan in charge of passenger-car design and increased output to 270 units in 1937, 542 in 1938, and 372 in 1939. Alfa Romeos were elitist cars and when, after World War Two, Enzo Ferrari began making just such cars, he essentially created a new branch of the Alfa Romeo tradition with which he had lived for a good part of his life.

ALFA ROMEO IN WWII

Gobbato shaped Il Portello into one of Europe's leading producers of aero engines. He increased the size of the plant enormously and his payroll increased from less than 1000 employees in 1933 to more than 9500 in 1943. The operation was running so smoothly by 1938 that in April of that year he was able to undertake for the Ministry of Aeronautics the design and construction of a huge, ultra-modern factory at Pomigliano d'Arco, near Naples. It would be a branch of Alfa Romeo, devoted to the production of aero engines and complete aircraft. Gobbato presented the plans for the project that October and was present when Il Duce laid the cornerstone on the oddly chosen date of April 1, 1939. Foreseeably, the plant and its infrastructure were outstanding models of the most modern architectural and industrial techniques. Its productive life was rather meteoric. After being touched only lightly by Allied bombs in September 1943, it was systematically dynamited and razed to the ground by German military forces retreating from the south.

Having the Nazi German military *in casa* probably was

The central foundry after the bombing mission. Below: Gobbato.

the major incentive for the overthrow of the Fascist government by its own subjects on July 25, 1943. But the Germans seized control of two-thirds of the country and on, September 8, they set Mussolini up as the head of a puppet government. This event sparked the formal beginning of the great Italian Resistance movement: war against the occupying ally-turned-tyrant.

Gobbato remained serenely at the helm of his company, which had been placed under German military command. He was motivated by a sole sense of duty: to the greatest extent possible, to save the company, its property and its personnel, as his chief role in the salvation of his country. Gobbato spoke German fluently and was one of the rather small number of Italians that the German command respected and would listen to; through diplomacy and skill he brought his vast organization through the Occupation almost totally intact. It was Gobbato who created the intellectual, philosophical, and industrial base for the organization that would flower after his death. With Gobbato's approval, his man Ricart was responsible for the creation of the Satta equipe, which would determine on the technical level the course which Alfa would follow after World War Two. However, there was nothing he could do about the Allied bombings that touched the plant at Il Portello in 1943 and reduced almost all of it to rubble on October 29, 1944. Like the leader that he was, he coped, as best he could.

The liberation of Italy from the Nazi yoke nominally took place on April 25, 1945, and the Italian Resistance took immediate power. It was the long awaited moment for the settling of old accounts, and there were isolated charges that Gobbato had collaborated criminally with the Germans. Twice on April 27 he was tried by People's Courts — the improvised justice of the moment — and twice he was absolved of any guilt by these tribunals, which existed largely to condemn. Then, on the morning of the 28th, as he was walking from Il Portello to his nearby home, a blue Lancia Augusta braked to a stop near him and he saluted its occupants, whom he obviously knew. Two got out, one with a tommy gun, the other with a shotgun, and riddled him where he stood. They then rode away and, although there had been witnesses, the assassins never were apprehended. It was a bitter end to a career which had been of boundless general and national service.

Ugo Gobbato stood about five-foot, nine-inches, had

1939 Alfa Romeo 8C 2900B spyder, by Touring, owned by John Mozart.

brown eyes and hair and was of a slightly stocky build. He spoke five languages in addition to his native Italian: English, French, German, Russian, and Spanish. His son, Pierugo, an athletic 70 when I interviewed him in 1988, still remembers him with awe and love. In spite of his own very successful career, which includes the managing directorship of Ferrari in 1965 and '66 and an important role at Lancia from 1969 through '76, he says with all candor:

''I always regarded my father's example as being unapproachable by ordinary human beings. Even if I may have had certain satisfactions in my work, they are as nothing in comparison with what my father was able to achieve.

''He was infinitely kind. He taught me '*sempre la testa sopra il cuore*' — 'always the head over the heart.' He meant 'never let yourself be carried away by sentiment; always rely on reason.' But he was constantly moved by sentiment. A super-technician, he also had the soul of a poet, as his drawings hint. He was a dreamer, always. At the same time, he was intensely self-disciplined and had a perhaps too strong sense of duty. I cannot remember ever having had an evening meal at home with my father. He never got home before 9:30 or 10:00, and he also worked on Sundays. He never should have gone to Il Portello on that fatal morning, but he felt that he must do it. That was his destiny.''

KPE
842

CHAPTER 7

GIOACHINO COLOMBO

Gioachino Colombo
1903-1987
Chief Designer

MILLE MACCHINE ho fatto! A thousand machines I've made—more than Bugatti, who only made a hundred and eight!'' Gioachino Colombo was 61 years old when he confided these statistics to me in 1964, looking across his desk in the headquarters of motorcycle manufacturer Meccanica Verghera. He was short, just a bit rotund, bald, and full of high-strung vitality. Colombo was a very serious professional who nevertheless laughed with easy spontaneity in talking about his three decades at the vortex of Alfa Romeo race-car engineering, with time out to design the original Ferrari V-12 engine. His precise memory for even the smallest technical details was astonishing.

Colombo was born at Legnano, about 20 miles northwest of Milano, on January 9, 1903. Enzo Ferrari somehow picked up the idea that he had graduated from engineering school in Switzerland. Actually, he had begun his career at the tender age of fourteen, learning to be a mechanical draftsman at the Officine Franco Tosi, a famous manufacturer in his home town. There he acquired wide experience, including exposure to diesel engines and steam turbines. Very gifted, he won a competitive examination given by the Società Italiana Nicola Romeo and, early in 1924, found himself a member of the little task force being put together by Jano for the creation of the P2. Although he was twenty-one, he left the impression with Jano of having been ''a little boy.'' His chief found him to be intelligent, alert, nimble and fast and in 1928, young Colombo was promoted to head of the drawing office, handling not only passenger cars, but racing cars as well, when the need for them arose. As chief engineering draftsman, his responsibilities were great, including rendering his boss's ideas feasible from

every standpoint and making them beautiful to boot.

As Alfa Romeo grew, producing aero engines and trucks, as well as cars, technical director Jano spent increasingly less time at the drawing board. After 1932 or '33, he could devote only a small part of his time to racing and, he said, "Colombo began to be my right arm."

The transfer of racing operations to Scuderia Ferrari in Modena enabled practically all of the Portello personnel to concentrate upon commercial production. An exception was Colombo, who served as engineering liaison between the two centers of the Jano school of design. As long as Jano was the top man, all of the products of that school were attributed to him, regardless of the contributions made by others, including Colombo, who no doubt merits a great deal of credit which he never received. As for that which he did receive, it is confused and contradictory. The *Milleruote* encyclopedia, for example, credits him unquali-

1938/1950 Alfa Romeo G.P. 158, owned by the Alfa Romeo Museo. Below: a cutaway of the car in its 158 fitting, with a single-stage supercharger.

fiedly with the design of the Types 158, 308, 312, and 316. This is important indeed, considering the great postwar significance of the 158. However Fusi, a witness, does not state in his "bible" that Colombo was the author of any particular designs, but merely that he was sent to Modena in May, 1937 to work on the above named projects and that he returned to Il Portello in 1939. A look at the cars themselves throws a good deal of light on this subject.

THE TIPO 158

The number designation of course represents 1.5 liters and eight cylinders. A new international Grand Prix formula was to go into effect in 1938, limiting supercharged engines to three liters' displacement. Moreover, the Royal Automobile Club of Italy planned to base the national championship upon voiturette racing—cars of 1500 cc blown—the following year, although this, too, became effective in 1938. Ferrari apparently had the idea of creating a new 1500 for the Royal Automobile Club of Italy circuit, which also could provide pieces for an imposing car to fit the new GP formula. Early in 1937 he obtained Ing. Gobbato's approval for such a project, to be carried out at Ferrari's own race shops in Modena. His request for the loan of Gioachino Colombo to direct the engineering side of the program was granted, and the factory also supplied an excellent draftsman, Angelo Nasi.

Ferrari himself probably had a lot to say about what he wanted in these cars, depending heavily upon the counsel of Luigi Bazzi, whom he later called the project's "foremost collaborator." He denied any contribution by Jano, of which there apparently was none in the sense of direct

personal participation. Nasi, in addition to doing the general drafting, is credited with the design of the 158's steering and front suspension. Ferrari employee Federico Giberti designed other parts, and Alberto Massimino has been named as author of the car's transmission and rear axle. Ferrari was generous with his credit to these men; as for the fundamental parenthood of the 158 he wrote, "It is the intellectual patrimony of Gioachino Colombo and Luigi Bazzi." It was designed and fabricated at the Scuderia in Modena. At a later stage, cylinder block castings would be made at the Portello, but the original cylinders were built up out of steel. The lathe operator who machined the barrels from billets was Reclus Forghieri, father of the young Ferrari engineer to come.

The new car was called the Alfetta, that having been the nickname of the original overhead-camshaft 6C 1500. According to Fusi, its engine and chassis treatment were traditional Alfa, which is to say Jano. The trailing-arm transverse-leaf front suspension was similar to that already used on Alfa ifs sixes and eights. The rear suspension by swing axle and transverse leaf, along with the transaxle at the rear, were patterned after the 8C 2900. Following "Jano" ifs practice, Porsche suspension was employed. The cam followers and blower were identical to those of

Above: Emilio Villoresi, who was killed testing the 158. Right: Farina driving the 158 in 1947, at Monza. Bottom: The eight-cylinder 158 engine; and the carburetor designed especially for the 158.

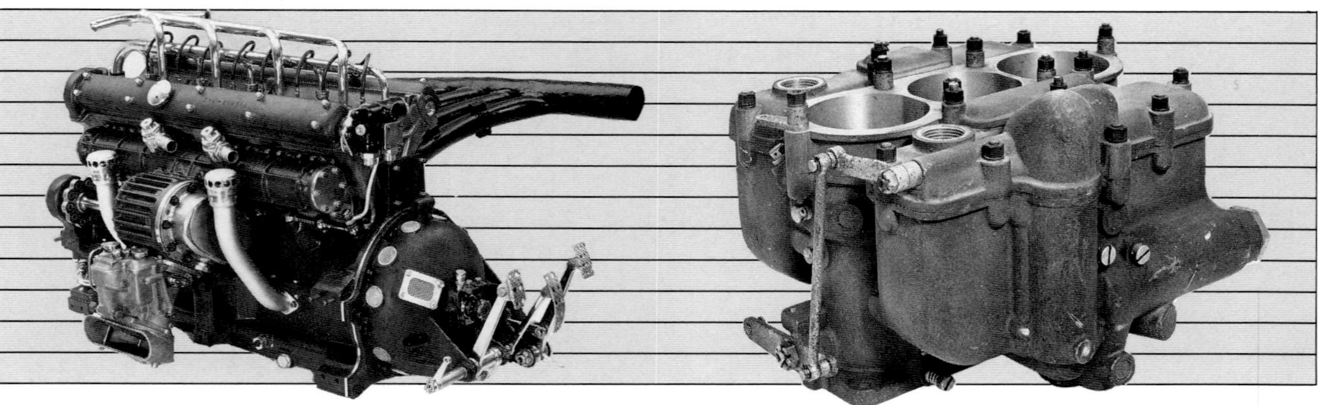

that car. Innovations were the lowering of the drive shaft and thus of the car's center of gravity by means of supplementary gears; use of sliding supports for the cross-springs; and adoption of a single block for the eight cylinders, with the camshaft and accessory drive moved from the center of the engine to the front, in the interest of — Colombo said—making the engine as short as possible.

This Roots-blown, 1479 cc power plant developed 131 bhp per liter during its first season, 1938. This figure was an all-time high for the marque, up to that time. The car took 1st, 2nd, and 7th in its first race, at Livorno on August 8, after which its reliability went to hell and two cars were involved in accidents that were fatal to their drives.

Four improved cars were built for 1939, and the combination began to work. The season began with a 3rd at Tripoli; then a 1st, 3rd, and 5th in the Coppa Ciano; 2nd, 3rd, and 4th in the Coppa Acerbo; and 1st and 2nd in class in the Swiss GP at Berne. When the 158 concluded its prewar career in the Tripoli GP in May 1940, it swept the top three places, which was the sort of thing that Ferrari had in mind. The little engine had been persuaded to yield 152 bhp per liter. That was the all-time record for single stage supercharged Alfas, but only the beginning of what was to come after the war.

The car itself is an embodiment of the axiom that success has many fathers, failure none.

"*Fatto Colombo*!"—done by Colombo! the man himself exulted as he flourished his signature across the bottom of a drawing of the Alfetta engine.

"*E un motore mio*!"—It's one of *my* engines, Jano said firmly and with pride, seeing the drawing framed and hanging on the wall of my study, royally ignoring the signature of his understudy.

In early editions of his memoirs Ferrari spoke of the 158 as "one of my personal ideas, realized through my desire." In the 1980 edition, he described the car as "a racing machine entirely 'mine'."

And there are those in Spain who look upon Wifredo Ricart as the father of the 158. Each has his own way of interpreting the facts. No living person knows the exact roles played by Ferrari, Bazzi, Nasi, Giberti and Colombo on projects on which they worked together at Modena. Luigi Fusi gives Ferrari much credit for ideas for the 158, but he is emphatic that the person on the drawing pencil throughout was Colombo."

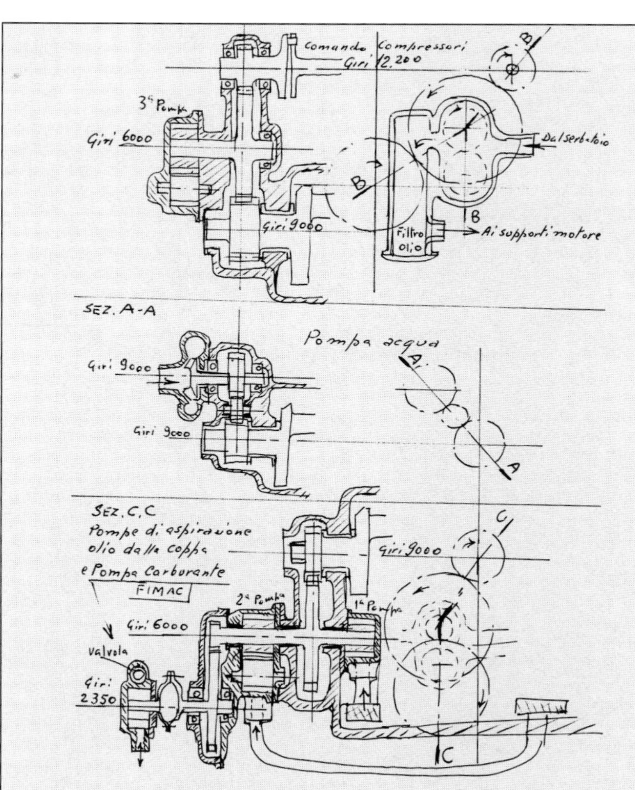

Above: the 158 in 1938. Left: A drawing in Colombo's own hand, sketched during a discussion with the author on the subject of the 158. Below: the 1938 Tipo 316 motor.

THE TIPO 316

The first project undertaken at Scuderia Ferrari once the 158 engine had entered the development stage was the first of three challengers for the new three-liter formula. Its engine was a two-crankshaft U-16. Its cylinder blocks were set fairly far apart and splayed at sixty degrees, in order to provide space for the pair of large Roots blowers which were mounted between them in a very hot location. This cumbersome idea dated back to Bugatti in 1917 and was very similar to the Stutz Black Hawk LSR engine, which had been concocted a decade before by Frank Lockhart out of a pair of 1500 cc straight eights made by Harry Miller. According to Fusi, the 316

Opposite page: 1933 Alfa Romeo 1900 Gran Turismo, owned by the Alfa Romeo Museo. This page: 1938 Alfa Romeo 8C 2900B Mille Miglia spyder, owned by Brooks Stevens.

engine was developed by Alberto Massimino, using two complete 158 engines except for their crankcases, which were replaced by a common one.

This power plant was installed directly into the chassis of the much-maligned Jano 12C 1937, the troubles with which had served at least as a pretext for putting an end to Jano's tenure at Alfa Romeo. Fusi reports that the mysterious troubles were quickly eliminated and that, when two of these chassis received the 316 engine, no significant changes had to be made to their suspension or to their unit rear axle/transmission assembly. Only the front-end sheet metal required reshaping in order to accommodate the broad, barrel shaped power plant.

One of these cars achieved very good lap times when driven by Clemente Biondetti in practice for the Tripoli GP in May 1938, only to be judged not sufficiently *a posto* to race. It took until September for this stage of their development to be reached, when they were driven in the Italian GP at Monza by Nino Farina and Biondetti. To the great credit of all concerned, they finished second and fourth, ahead of a pack of German cars, although first place was taken by Nuvolari's Auto Union and third by Caracciola's Mercedes. Then the 316 dropped out of sight until June 1939 and the Belgian GP at Spa-Francorchamps. Farina withdrew at about half distance with mechanical problems, and that ended the model's career. Precious little mileage had been realized out of a very ambitious and costly exercise.

THE TIPO 308

The next car in what turned out to be a series of efforts to find a key to the three-liter formula was the first to be built by the marque's new in-house racing department, Alfa Corse. While this organization replaced Scuderia Ferrari, with all of that entity's material being moved to Il Portello, it retained the services

Farina finishing first in a 158 at the GP at Silverstone.

Sommer in a Tipo 308 at the GP of Nizza, 1946.

of Enzo Ferrari as racing manager. The 308 engine was a very straightforward adaptation of the 8C 2900 to Grand Prix use, output being increased from 180 to 295 bhp. The chassis was an updating of the 1935 Tipo C, making the overall car a direct derivative of the P3 series, using a sleeker body with faired-in axles and suspension front and rear. Colombo was in charge of the modifications, which were numerous and important.

Two 308s made their debut in practice for the Pau GP in April 1938. Driving one of them, Nuvolari broke the lap record, only to have his car burst into flame, due to a defective fuel-tank mounting. His car was destroyed and that of teammate Emilio Villoresi, which risked the same fate, was withdrawn. This was the first race of the three-liter formula and it may have been the revelation of overwhelming German superiority, rather than his burns, that caused Nuvolari to announce his retirement from racing. He was back in the saddle in July, but the marque he drove for was Auto Union.

Two 308s took the start in the Tripoli GP, a month after Pau. Eugenio Siena hit a wall with his car and was killed. Raymond Sommer drove the sister machine into fourth place, trailing a trio of Mercedes. They had a crushing 36 percent more horsepower than the straight-eight Alfa, which was seen no more in prewar circuit racing. In Sommer's hands, however, it did win the three-liter class in the La Turbie hill climb in both 1938 and '39. Out of wartime mothballs, in the late Forties it cut a modest swath for itself in Europe and Argentina, in the hands of Sommer, Varzi, and Wimille.

1938 Alfa Romeo Special 308C, owned by Indianapolis Speedway Hall of Fame Museum.

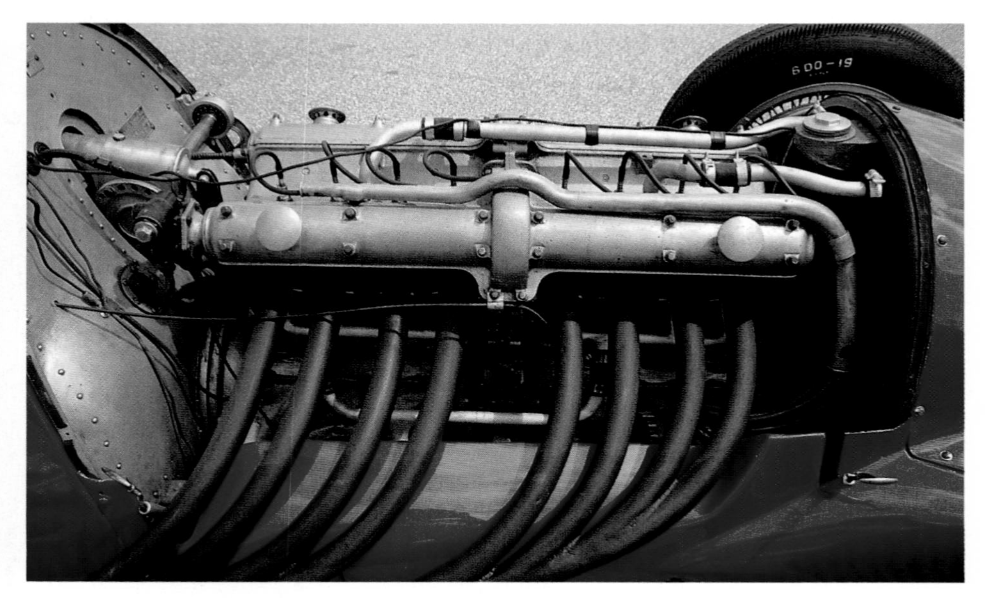

On June 18, 1940, veteran Alfa test driver Attilio Marinoni was killed on the Milan-Varese autostrada when his car, a modified 158 with 512 suspension components, collided with a truck.

first dynamometer test March 12, 1940 and, once sorted out, gave a reported 490 bhp at 7800 rpm. This was equal to 164 bhp per liter, versus 149 for the existing Massimino-prepared 16-cylinder Tipo 316. If true, it was the highest specific output in history, except for that of the brand-new Mercedes-Benz M 165 1.5-liter V-8.

In the running-gear department, Ricart introduced a De Dion rear axle, with four-speed transmission in unit with the final-drive housing. Rear suspension was by longitudinal torsion bars, with coil spring independent suspension at the front. The complete car began to run on April 19, 1940, one of the many precise dates that can be fixed thanks to Busso's practice of keeping a detailed daily journal. The car was beginning to get sorted out when, less than eight weeks later, on June 10, Italy entered World War II.

The Tipo 512 engine had much in common with that of the 162, with the major structural difference that it was a flat twelve. Its bore and stroke was 54 x 54.2 mm (2.126 x 2.134 inches), for a displacement of 1490 cc. The shortness of the stroke set a new all-time record. The vertically split block/crankcase castings were magnesium, again with wet liners and detachable heads. This time Ricart used only two valves per cylinder, still with finger followers and mousetrap springs. The two camshafts per bank were driven by a train of spur gears at the front. The rod and internal main bearings (six) were rollers, with a plain bearing at each end of the crankshaft. Two-stage supercharging was employed again, this time with one low- and one high-pressure Roots blower, each with two lobes, and a single triple-throat downdraft carburetor. This engine, laid out by Special Projects Chief Draftsman Ettore Pagani, also was a gorgeous piece of sculptural architecture. Ricart conceived all his engines to be that way.

The 512 powerplant ran in the assembled chassis for the first time September 10, 1940, coming to life in a nation at war. Its output was 335 bhp at 8600 rpm. This was a staggering 225 bhp per liter, as opposed to the 152 that the Alfetta had been persuaded to yield for what there was of that year's racing season. By comparison, the two-stage blown Mercedes-Benz M 165 of the previous year had developed 186 bhp per liter. If the figures are at all realistic—

Right: Ricart driving the Tipo 162 prototype as it leaves for its first road test in June, 1940. Below: Pratt and Whitney Wasp Major engine: 18,679 of this 28-cylinder powerplant were built from 1945-1955. Hailed as a great achievement, it vindicated the confidence of Ricart and Gobbato in the 1101.

and there is no reason to doubt them—Ricart set a record for internal-combustion engine output that exceeded by far anything in the history of the art. Perhaps Gobbato's faith in his talent had not been misplaced.

This engine occupied a rear-central location in its tubular chassis and was separated from the cockpit by a huge, saddle-shaped fuel tank that fit the driver like an armchair. A five-speed transmission extended aft of the output centerline of a De Dion rear end. Axle torque reactions were controlled by diagonal radius rods that formed a triangle with the extremities of the De Dion tube and a frame-mounted central pivot located well to the rear. The parallelogram ifs, as well as the rear suspension, used longitudinal torsion bars as a springing medium. It also employed three-shoe brakes, another Ricart innovation. (The principle worked so well in later Alfa passenger-car practice that early disc brakes were no match for it.)

The 512 monoposto was given its first workout on September 12, 1940, three months after Italy's entry into the war. The man at the wheel was the phenomenal Consalvo Sanesi, who had taken over as Alfa Romeo's chief test driver following the death that year of veteran drive Attilio Marinoni on the Milan-Varese autostrada on June 18. This brings up another inexactitude in Ferrari's sometimes slanted recollections. He says in his autobiography that Marinoni met his end driving one of Ricart's 512s powered by a 158 engine. This combination fits the facts awkwardly, physically as well as chronologically. Others close to the tragic incident say that the car in question was an Alfetta that had been fitted experimentally with 512 rear, and perhaps front, suspension. Of what the car consisted may be irrelevant. According to Ricart's sons, the accident was caused by a head-on collision with a truck whose driver had apparently dozed off. The common denominator in the two stories is that the 512, along with the rest of Ricart's serious designs for Alfa, was eminently unroadworthy. Sanesi told me that, although the 512 had an advantage of more than 100 bhp over the Alfetta, he could lap Monza two seconds faster in the less powerful car. The 512's handling was simply a disaster.

One of Ricart's serious handicaps, according to Satta, was his strong spontaneous resistance to any criticism of ideas that were dear to him. Sanesi tried to explain his seat-of-the-pants analysis of the problem. Not without some reason, Ricart was convinced that he was the object of a conspiracy to make the Alfetta look good and his own brainchild look bad. Then one day Sanesi asked Emilio Degiuseppe, head of assembly in Experimental, to give him a hand. Degiuseppe was a huge bear of a man and very powerful, and when Sanesi asked him to grab the two front

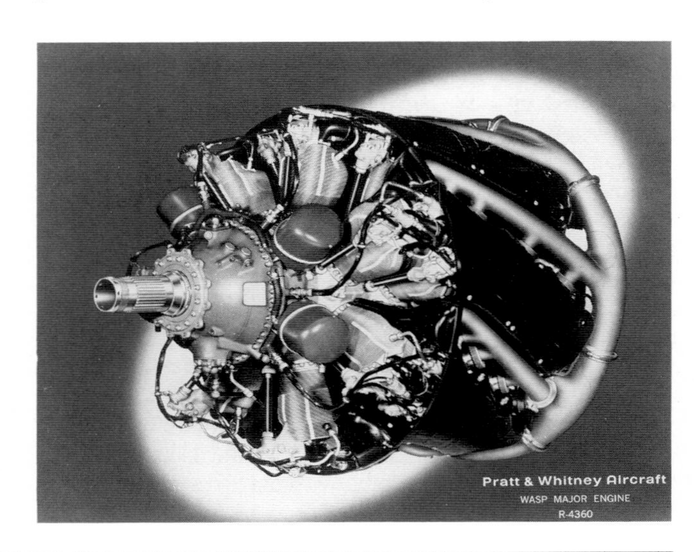

wheels and see what he could find in the way of play and give, the whole front end almost fell apart. Ricart, called to examine the results, realized that Sanesi had been feeding him correct information all along, and relations improved between these two men.

At some time in 1941, Ricart and his team produced a design called the Tipo 163. It was a competition coupe powered by the 16-cylinder 162 engine, in this case mounted rear-centrally and drastically detuned for endurance. The prototype never was completed and never ran, due to the forthcoming evacuation of Ricart's staff from Milan. Although the 163 design used coil springs all around, its suspension geometry had everything in common with that of its sister cars. The bad handling inherent in all these chassis became perfectly understandable, Busso says, as soon as he and his aernoautics-trained teammates learned about the finer points of chassis design. The problem was a roll axis that was completely aberrant. The rival, veteran team no doubt knew this but kept its know-how to itself.

Ricart's magnum opus while with Alfa Romeo was his aero engine, the Tipo 1101. It was a liquid-cooled radial with seven banks of four cylinders each, for a total of 28 cylinders and a global displacement of 50 liters. In general architecture it was reminiscent of the similar engine that Edmund Rumpler had visualized for his projected transatlantic air transports in the Twenties, and Ricart had longer-range plans for a 42-cylinder version, using seven rows of six cylinders. The great advantage of the configuration was its small diameter and therefore greatly reduced frontal area and drag. While the 1000-hp Pegasus had a diameter of 55.3 inches and a similar Fiat 52.6, the Ricart AR 1101 measured just 44.9 inches across.

Orazio Satta begain assigning calculations for this engine to Busso on November 7, 1939, and Ettore Pagani did the layout drawings. It was a more than formidable task, and it was not until July 19, 1941 that the first variant ran: a

The turbocharged version of Ricart's 28-cylinder, 50-liter Tipo 1101 aero engine was expected to produce about 2500 bhp.

Right and opposite page, below: Renderings of two projected body configurations for the Gazzella. Below: The Gazzella sedan proposal.

single-bank four-cylinder module followed by an inverted V-8 made up of two of the same banks. The first 28-cylinder engine was completed at year's end, and it began to run its test rig on January 3, 1942. Development resulted in the achievement, on November 26, of an output of about 2000 horsepower, making it one of the most powerful aero engines of all time. This was not enough for Ricart, who then designed an ingenious turbocharging system which, had it ever been built, should have boosted the engine's output to somewhere around 2500 bhp. . .at 23,000 feet.

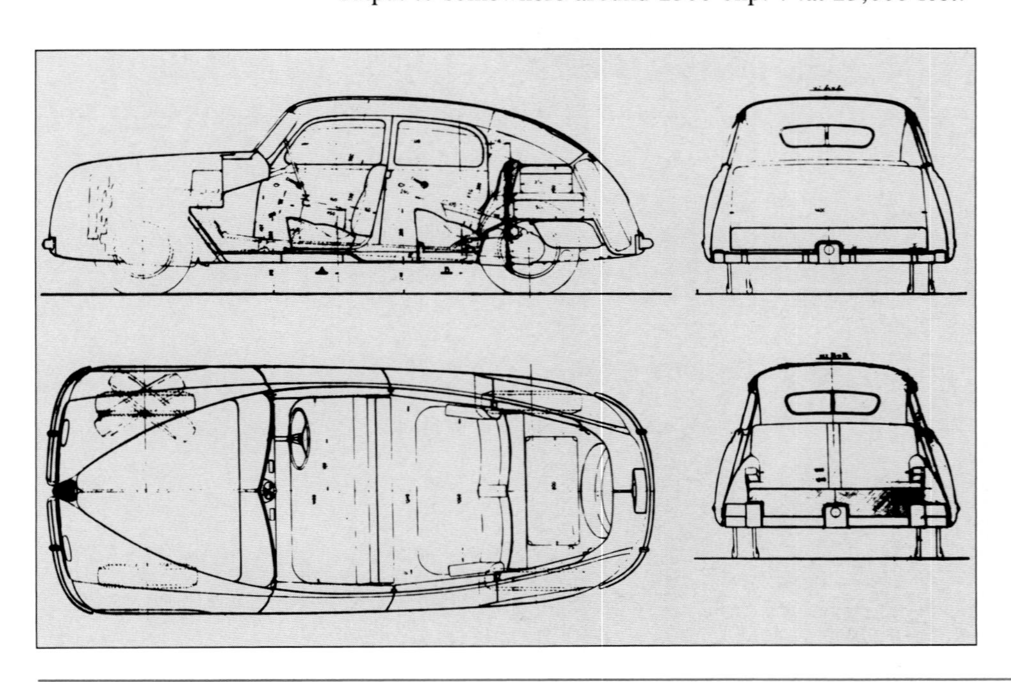

On October 24, 1942, the first significant Allied bombing of Milan took place. Portello was not touched and few suspected at the time that this marked the beginning of the end for Northern Italian industry, as it was for the work of Wifredo Ricart. Then on November 19 came the first heavy bombing of Turin. In its wake came the great evacuations of people and of industrial operations from main target areas. On December 2, Ricart announced to his staff that all Special Projects, Design and Experimental personnel were being moved to the Lago d'Orta, in the hinterland north of Milano and just a handful of miles west of Lego Maggiore. By January 4 many of them and their families had settled into the old Albergo Belvedere at the town of Orta, overlooking the lake. Alfa had a largo aeronautical experimental center at nearby Arimeno, also on the lake; much equipment was moved there, including the parts for 20 1101 engines. Food was scarce, but work went on. A wealthy Alfista offered an underground hiding place for the Alfettas and 512s, so they could be sequestered in abolsute secrecy; this effort was helped by the fact that no one wanted the responsibility of knowing where they were.

All this happened none too soon, for on February 14, 1943, the Portello factory took a heavy rain of Allied bombs. Work to perfect the 1101 continued, under difficult conditions, The war went badly for the Italians and on July 25 Mussolini resigned; political chaos and violence broke out everywhere and the German forces of occupation settled in. Bands of Resistance fighters (Partigiani), German soldiers and Fascists took turns descending upon Orta, with frequent extortions and kidnappings. The Germans wanted manpower and brainpower for their factories at home, and Ricart had to fight to keep his staff together. Edo Masoni,

the feel of the car in the hands of he who drives it. Those things always have been a tradition with us, a thing that we always have sought to provide in our cars."

The other tradition stems from the company's activity as a major producer of aircraft engines — a decade of highly specialized experience which ended with the bombing of the Il Portello works in Milan on October 1944. Of those days Satta said:

"Aeronautical technology had, over automotive technology, the great superiority of the necessity of absolute reliability and thus the need for much greater planning and application. It required concepts of a much more developed and sophisticated technical character because, naturally, the reliability and therefore the safety of an aircraft should be as absolute as possible. Beyond that, all of the branches of science and technology which were necessary for keeping abreast in aero engines were, for me and all of us, a very important school. This is why, when we had finished with aero engines at the end of the war, we were able to transfer all those systems to the design of new automobiles. I think that it was done at just the right time."

At that epoch, aside from engine design, only in Germany and the USA had a small amount of real science been applied to the design of the automobile as a whole. When it was decided that Alfa Romeo should resume automotive activity, one of Satta's early initiatives was the setting up of a program for scientific research on vehicle dynamics. In doing this, he had from the outset the collaboration of a highly trained young graduate engineer named Erwin Landsberg. Taking the existing 6C 2500 as a base, they started from various conditions of tire loading under acceleration, braking, and cornering and calculated them back to all parts of the car. A growing body of important new knowledge of a scientific nature was accumulated in this way. It went into the design of the Alfa Romeo 1900: a most outstanding all-new vehicle. It was all Satta — and was the parent of all subsequent passenger cars designed and built at Il Portello and at the new factory at nearby Arese.

The 1900 was the embodiment of the basic Satta concept of what a volume-produced Alfa Romeo should be. It should have the performance characteristics upon which much of the marque's reputation rested. It should not be too expensive. Up to this point, the grand maximum of components for cars of the marque had been manufactured, at great cost, by the company itself. This included such elements

1938 8C 2900B sport coupe, winner of the 1948 Grand Prix at Watkins Glen, owned by Arthur Jacobs.

The Tipo 158 in 1946, just after being removed from storage. Gathered for the event are (from left) engineers Giampaolo Garcea, Gaboardi, Giuseppe Busso, Livio Nicolis, Guidotti, Consalvo Sanesi, Managing Director Enrico Magnaghi, Trossi and Varzi.

as shock absorbers, brakes, clutch, steering, and so on. Now the product, while retaining its traditional character, should utilize the greatest possible number of components made by leading specialists: clutches by Borg & Beck, brakes by Girling, bearings by Vandervell, etc. It should be mechanically simple, which favored the choice of the four-cylinder engine. Weight should be kept at the lowest reasonable level, and this for Satta meant aircraft-type monocoque construction. He knew that discipline already and he demanded and obtained optimum torsional rigidity in the new body-frame structure. Here, as elsewhere, he was very much of a pioneer.

Satta favored fairly small cars and consistently sought the smallest external dimensions, along with the greatest possible internal space. Aside from the fact that more bulky cars cost and weigh more, Satta saw them as being unsuited to Italian road conditions, and in the beginning Italy was his all-important market. Cars designed to his thinking should be fairly narrow, as well as not too long. Narrowness, while contributing to nimbleness and ease of handling on Italy's abundant narrow roads, also favored efficient penetration of the air. Of course Satta had a thorough scientific grounding in aerodynamics and made early use of wind tunnel testing.

Just as the spirited performance made possible by a close power-to-weight ratio was fundamental to the concept, so was outstanding roadholding. This made suspension an object for scientific analysis from the start. Within the frame of reference of cost, simplicity, and light weight, the rigid rear axle was found to be unbeatable, and became a hallmark of the school. When even better roadholding could be afforded at higher cost, the Alfetta's De Dion rear axle perpetuated the geometry of the rigid type, while reducing unsprung weight to the ultimate minimum.

Another fundamental factor in Satta's design philosophy was safety and here, too, he was a pioneer. The Giulia, for example, was one of the world's first cars to have a safety body, in the modern sense of designed-in crushability. Satta conceived it as being very rigid in the passenger compartment, but soft at front and rear. The Giulia also had its steering gearbox mounted on the bulkhead, behind the engine, and not in the usual farforward position. These steps and many like them were taken well before American safety regulations became effective in 1966. When the Giulia crash-test program was begun, very few modifications had to be made to the car in order for it to meet those draconian requirements. Satta innovated never for the sake of innovation, but only for that of genuine improvement. He was not bound to any given configuration of automotive architecture and, at the time of his final illness, in the early Seventies, had led his team deeply into the development of a transverse-engine, front-wheel-drive, mid-size car that would have the roadholding of an Alfa Romeo.

In spite of the monumental importance of his technical and creative leadership, Orazio Satta shunned personal credit and would not speak of his own contributions. Instead, he gave total credit for the achievements of his administration to the design group which was responsible to him, and to the excellent talents which supported that group. It consisted of just five men: Garcea, Busso, Colucci, Nicolis, and Sanesi, which is the order in which he listed them to me in 1970. Of them he said: "These men and their co-workers are the strength of Alfa Romeo."

Each is very important and merits being known.

Left: (left to right): Nicolis, Satta and Busso. Below: Garcea in 1985. Bottom left: The six-cylinder 2500 motor of 1948. Bottom right: 1947 6C 2500 Freccia d'Oro.

GIAMPAOLO GARCEA

Giampaolo Garcea was born at Padova on 10 June 1912, and there received his degree in mechanical engineering in 1934. Jobs were very difficult for young engineers to obtain at the time and, owing to his academic qualifications, he won an Alfa Romeo scholarship at the Politecnico di Torino where, a year later, he received his degree in aeronautical engineering. He and Satta were classmates there, and they became close friends.

As soon as he received his second university degree, Garcea wrote to Alfa's Managing Director, Ing. Ugo Gobbato, saying that he had completed his studies, thanks to the company's generosity; he furthermore offered his services, should they ever be required. To his delight and surprise, he was hired immediately. Thus, in August 1935, at the age of 23, he began work at Il Portello, assigned to the aero engine department.

There he worked under department head Amleto Bossi, perhaps the firm's first great specialist in experimentation with development and testing of engines. Bossi had started with Alfa as a simple workman in 1911, but his remarkable intelligence and productivity of ideas had enabled him to rise to his important level. Garcea expected this veteran to make life difficult for him, a rank newcomer with a head full of book-lore, but he was wrong. Bossi received him with open arms and willingly passed on everything he knew. This was Garcea's first real taste of the remarkable team

Right: 1950 6C 2500 SS Villa d'Este coupe, owned by the Alfa Romeo Museo. Opposite: above: 1955 Guilietta four-door Berlina Tipo 750C, owned by the Alfa Romeo Museo. Below: 1954 1900 Sport Spider, owned by the Alfa Romeo Museo.

spirit which prevailed at Il Portello.

The company had been manufacturing a small, seven-cylinder radial engine which Vittorio Jano had designed, but it was obsolescent at birth. To correct this situation, Alfa acquired a license to build the avant-grade Bristol Pegasus which, somewhat modified, resulted in the extraordinarily dependable AR 126 and 128. Ing. Gobbato also had engaged ex-Isotta Fraschini engineer Giustino Cattaneo who, using the Pegasus as a base, produced the two-row radial AR 135, a marvel of its day. Garcea was co-responsible for the development of these three engines, which became the main stock-in-trade of the firm, in response to growing military demand. Automotive production dwindled to a trickle of ten cars in 1936.

Cattaneo and Gobbato did not get along, the former leaving Alfa in 1935. Gobbato probably had reason on his side in that case, as he had when Vittorio Jano left two years later. To fill the gap created by this critical exodus, Gobbato engaged Spanish automotive and aeronautical engineer Wifredo Ricart, who was known particularly for his organizational ability. One of its early expressions was his establishment of a new Design and Experimental Department, which he headed. Under this department were separate Design and Experimental services, each with its own various aeronautical, truck, gasoline engine, diesel, and automotive sections. Garcea continued in his good position in the Experimental Service. Ricart also established a Special Studies Service, attached to his Design Service. To head it be hired a brilliant, 27-year-old teaching assistant away from the Politecnico di Torino: Orazio Satta. Thus Garcea and his old friend were reunited, and the nucleus was formed for the creative team to come at Alfa. It would include Romolo Gatti and, eventually, Filippo Surace and Livio Nicolis. All of these men had been students of three then-famous luminaries of the Politechnico di Torino: Panetti and Albenga for aerodynamics, and Capetti for inter-

Alfa Romeo

Above: Consalvo Sanesi in a Tipo 158.
Below: Colucci in 1985.

year before he was to reach retirement age, Busso severed all ties with the company. He continues to live in Arese and his relationship with Alfa has been positively renewed.

IVO COLUCCI

Ivo Colucci was the other of Satta's top two men in Design. His specialty was body engineering — both structural and styling. Satta himself happened to be strong in both of these fields and was consulted much more by Colucci than by Busso, to whom Satta gave much more free play. But Colucci was a top treater of sheet metal and, as such, an essential and precious member of this small but very creative team.

Colucci was born at Livorno, on 30 September, 1914 and went to work at Il Portello in 1932 as a worker in the body-building section of the factory. In 1935 he entered the special shop reserved for the construction of experimental coachwork, where he served as a draftsman. In 1937 he was transferred to the main body design office, where he continued to work as a draftsman until 1940, when wartime conditions caused him to be moved to the Cantieri Riuniti dell'Adriatico at Monfalcone. There Colucci began to acquire the knowledge of aircraft fuselage design which would prove to be so valuable when the time came to develop the monocoque structure for the Alfa Romeo 1900.

From Monfalcone, Colucci went on to the huge aircraft factory which Alfa Romeo had constructed recently at Pomigliano d'Arco, near Naples. There he worked as an aircraft draftsman under Ing. Raimondo Gatti, another alumnus of the Turin Polytechnic and friend of Satta. When that plant was destroyed many of the employees, including Gatti and Coluccci, were transferred to another company facility, this one at Armeno, in the hills above the Lago d'Orta, just west of Lago Maggiore.

A great part of the design and experimental departments had been decentralized to this location. At Armeno, Gatti and Colucci were assigned officially to military and aeronautical projects; in reality they worked on products which the company might produce should events prevent the production of vehicles and engines. They developed such potential merchandise as sheet-metal shutters and cabinets, and electrical domestic appliances.

When the automotive body-design office was re-established in 1946, Gatti and his right-hand man, Colucci, were integrated into it. It was under Gatti's direction that the two versions of series-built coachwork for the 6C 2500 Freccia d'Oro were realized, and the first small models for a future monocoque car were submitted to static testing by Garcea. Then Gatti left the company and, at the beginning of 1948, the capable Colucci took over as chief of body engineering. His first prototype for the future 1900 berlina was completed in the spring of 1950, to be followed by its line of ever more refined descendants.

Ivo Colucci no doubt was admired by Satta for his extreme modesty, as well as for his professional ability and solid contributions to Alfa Romeo. He became manager of his department in 1954 and bore the title of director when he left the company in 1977.

LIVIO NICOLIS

Livio Nicolis was born in Brescia on December 2, 1916. His family then moved to Verona and he did his first two years of engineering studies at nearby Padova. Because of his strong interest in aviation he went to Turin (in those days a degree in aeronautical engineering could be had only at the Polytechnic there and in Rome) and in 1940 he received a degree in mechanical and industrial engineering, sub-category aeronautical. He needed another year for his full aeronautical degree and registered for it, but the wartime situation suggested that he would do better to get into industry without delay. He applied at Alfa Romeo, was hired and assigned to the aero-engine experimental department — one of the places in the world where he would like most to be. His boss, Giampaolo Garcea, was just four-and-a-half years his elder, and the two men became fast friends from the first.

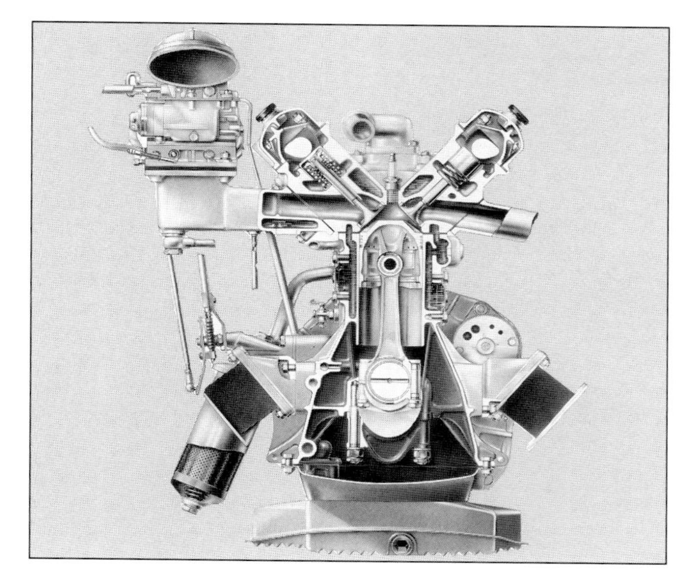

Top: 1962 Guilia SS. The 2000 motor, used from 1957 to 1962. Above: Livio Nicolis in 1985. Below left: 1954 2000 Sportiva prototype.

Above: 1961 Giulietta spyder, owned by Pietro Geranzani. Right: 1960 Giulietta Familiare station wagon, owned by the Alfa Romeo Museo.

Left: 1965 TZ 2 coupe, owned by Stephen Forristall. Middle: 1966 1600 spyder, Bottom: 1968 GT 1300 Junior coupe, owned by the Alfa Romeo Museo.

Opposite: Orazio Satta.

— and made an amazing recovery, but took his retirement in 1967, at the age of 56.

Orazio Satta Puliga was born in Turin on 6 October 1910. He took his degree in mechanical engineering at the Polytechnic there in 1933 and two years later had his degree in aeronautical engineering. With time out for military service as an artillery officer, he remained at the famous school as a teaching assistant in its aeronautics laboratory until 1939, when he joined Alfa Romeo. In 1946 he was appointed director of design and experimentation. In 1951 he became central director; in 1969 assistant general director. He also served as vice president of the Technical Commission of the CUNA.

Satta was a slender man of medium height, with dark eyes and olive complexion. He had very fine, powerful hands, as sculptors are supposed to have. The black hair of his youth turned silver in his fifties. He had an even, tranquil character and was known never to have raised his voice in anger. He spoke rapidly and eloquently. He had a good command of the English, French, and German languages and was well read in their technical literature. He was a person of culture who was widely admired for his human qualities and for his skill as a mediator. He was noted for being fair, just, and without pretension. Satta took a lively interest in all those who worked under him, all of whom he knew by their first names. He seemed to seek and inspire confidence and friendship in all of his human relations.

Sanesi, who exchanged these sentiments with Satta, feels that he was "too soft, too nice." This may reflect a certain failure in understanding the subtlety of the man. Ing. Landsberg agrees that he gave the impression of being flexible, but affirms that he was very tenacious and tough. He seems to have exerted considerable influence over top management. His ideas often were contested, but he seemed always to have such good evidence for their validity that they ended up being accepted. He might seem to yield in a dispute, only to come back to the same point later, with a different approach, and win it.

Landsberg feels that a very important element in Satta's career was his gift for what today is called systemic thinking: in an industry populated by specialists in this or that part of the whole, he consistently perceived each given motor vehicle as a global system. This seems to be reflected in the integrity of his products.

One of Satta's very remarkable achievements was the creation of a race of modern, mass-produced motor cars which, depending upon the model, retain or improve upon the competition-bred thoroughbred qualities of Alfa Romeos of the artisan past. Mentality and philosophy have everything to do with this phenomenon. Another contributing factor, Satta liked to emphasize, was the exacting discipline of aeronautical practice, which permeated his organization from top to bottom. Yet another element was the fact that, as Sanesi testifies, Satta was the most accomplished driver of the company's entire engineering staff. Nicolis refused to ride with Sanesi, but Satta was his serene, frequent passenger. It was routine for Sanesi to demonstrate a quirk of behavior at the limit, then say: "Now you do it, Ingegnere. You will see what I mean." And Satta would

1972 Montreal, owned by Count G. Lurani, with cutaway (above right).

do it very well, making the master tester's insights his own.

Orazio Satta died in Milano on March 1974, after a long and most difficult illness. His legacy is the post-World War II automotive tradition of Alfanord.

Engineer Satta is remembered with the greatest esteem as the last of the great individual design chiefs of Alfa Romeo. With his passing the firm's engineering department rapidly took on a highly modern ''team'' structure, guided successively by the individuals whom we shall meet next. Two of them led their ever-expanding departments for long periods, during which they acquired considerable fame. The last of the three has assumed leadership only recently and is now in the process of establishing his name.

A member of Alfa's present enormous engineering department is Orazio Satta's son Giuseppe.

1968 Carabo, owned by the Alfa Romeo Museo.

CHAPTER 10
THE MODERN ERA

Rudolf Hruska
Chief, design and experimentation
1915-

Filippo Surace
Chief Engineer
1928-

Domenico Chirico
Chief Engineer
1928-

Stefano Iacoponi
Chief Engineer
1941-

RUDI HRUSKA arrived at Alfa Romeo in 1951. He took his formal retirement 29 years later, but it was just that — a formality to be gone through at a certain age. Having done much to structure the company, his consulting services continued to be precious.

Although he is an extremely charismatic individual, this facet of Hruska's character never has been exploited, either by the company or by himself. It is a bonus item to be enjoyed by those who have occasion to deal with him. When I interviewed him at length in 1985 he recently had turned 70, but still was charged with overflowing energy. He works prodigiously, but does not permit work to interfere with keeping himself in excellent physical form. He has been very athletic all his life, and continues to run, swim, play tennis and ski. World War Two interrupted his plans to take up automobile racing very seriously, so that particular drive was diverted into his becoming a very fast and scientific test driver. He is a person of very broad culture, with well-developed interests in the various arts. He is a gourmet and an authority on exciting cuisine, and knows all manner of exotic recipes, which he enjoys preparing himself. He has a sophisticated knowledge of liquor and wines, but drinks sparingly and does not smoke. Hruska is slender, about five-feet-ten-inches tall, with dancing blue eyes and dark hair, shot with gray. He is a marvelously entertaining and stimulating speaker in German, Italian, French, and English. Dominating all of his other interests is his principal role in life, which is the creation of manufactured products and the tools, factories, and human organizations for making them. Extrovert that he is, he still does not seek publicity for himself but, if asked for his story, he recounts it,

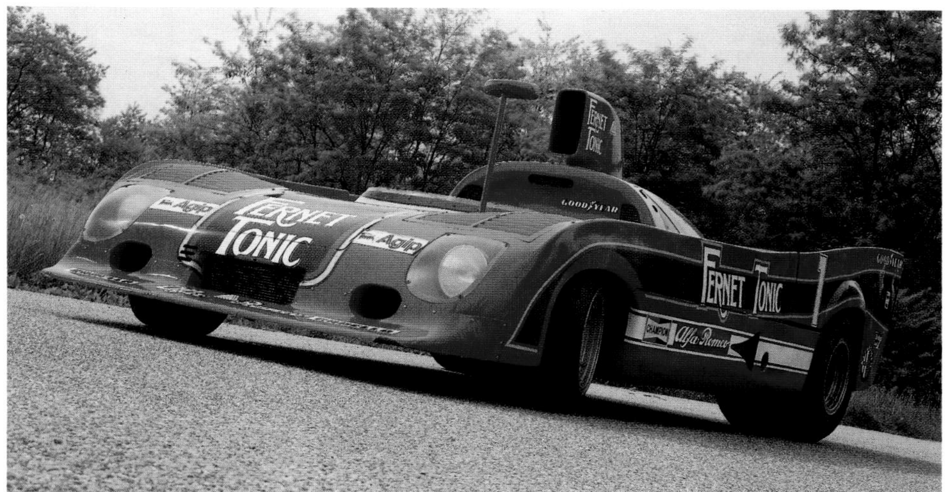

Top: 1977 33 SC 12, owned by the Alfa Romeo Museo. Above and left: 1982 Formula 1 racer, owned by the Alfa Romeo Museo.

Above: A 1968 architect's drawing of the new Alfasud plant at Pomigliano d'Arco. Below: Hruska.

the Italian financial world may be related to the fact that his fiancée was Luraghi's personal secretary. Lidia Bongiovanni could do more than take shorthand and type. She was one of Italy's top athletes, a member of the national ski team and an Olympic champion.

In any case, Luraghi became aware of Hruska's background, including his apprenticeship on the colossal Volkswagen undertaking. A Milanese himself, Luraghi took a special interest in the welfare of his ward at Il Portello. He and Finmeccanica needed a highly qualified presence on the spot. He offered the position to Hruska, who accepted and went to work on the Finmeccanica payroll as a technical consultant assigned to Alfa Romeo. To avoid any conflict of interest he resigned from his position as a Porsche representative, but on the most amicable of terms. It was understood that he would return to Porsche upon completion of the two-year Finmeccanica contract.

Hruska walked into Alfa when the original 1900 was in the midst of its teething problems. It was being produced at a rate of around 15 to 20 cars per day and constituted the marque's first venture into series production, even on this modest level. As excellent as the car was, it had many imperfections, and sales suffered in consequence. The situation was not surprising, given the fact that the men most responsible for the design—Ing. Orazio Satta and P.I. Giuseppe Busso—had most of their experience in the aeronautical field, and were treading on ground that was new to everyone at the factory. Full respect existed between them and Hruska, and under his guidance the considerably more refined Super 1900 series resulted. New production tooling which he introduced made the car more economical to build and, since it offered more quality for the money, its sales improved.

This was Hruska's first undertaking at Il Portello. Before it was well under way he began another, which was the reorganization of the plant for far more efficient volume production. Before this new regime could be properly set

Left: (left to right) Consalvo Sanesi, chief test driver; Domenico Chirico, Alfasud vehicle project chief; Heinrich Hoffman, Alfasud general manager; Hruska. Below: 1980 Alfasud ti 1.3-1.5; 1.5 Alfasud rally car engine.

in motion, he instigated a house-cleaning operation which was as draconian as it was herculean. The plant was full of useless, space-consuming stock which had been permitted to accumulate since the Thirties. This was the sort of rational reform that Hruska had been sent to identify the need for, and to effectuate. He received Luraghi's backing all the way.

The market for two-liter cars proved to be quite limited at that point in history, and so Alfa's goals were revised upward. Operation Giulietta was begun in 1952, with an objective of producing 200 cars per day. Hruska played a key role in the achievement of this figure and in even pushing it as high as 250 per day. I asked him what in his experience had equipped him to perform more than competently in dealing with such volumes. His answer was "Volkswagen, with its target of 1000 cars a day."

"But," I objected, "the VW never got into real production until well after the war, meaning that what you learned was chiefly theoretical."

"Look," said Hruska. "I took part in the basic planning of that immense operation, along with all of the persons responsible for the methods to be used in every sector of production. Ing. Porsche had gone to Dearborn and had discussed the project with old Mr. Ford, who took a sympathetic interest in it. Porsche asked Ford if he might have persons who were qualified in these various sectors, and who might be interested in coming to Germany to help with the creation of this new factory. It was with Ford's cooperation that over 30 men came, each an expert in his particular specialty. I worked with them and learned much of what they knew. The VW plant was no experiment for them. They did not have to spend time in discussion: they

Right: 1982 Alfasud Sprint Veloce 1500, owned by Cogliandro Lino. Below left: 1986 Milano four-door Berlina, owned by the Alfa Romeo Auto SpA. Below right: 1991 164, owned by Alfa Romeo of North America. Bottom: 1991 spyder, owned by Alfa Romeo of North America.

were certain of what they knew. You can be sure that the product would have been right, had it not been pushed aside by wartime needs.''

So it was Porsche, plus Ford, know-how, plus his own gifted thinking that Hruska brought to the Giulietta program. Everything was right, *da capo*, and the story of that car's astonishing success remains one of the high points in Italian automotive history. His contribution to it no doubt had much to do with his move to the Alfa Romeo payroll, as technical director of the company, responsible for all sectors of design, production, and quality.

One serious snag that arose early in the Giulietta project was external in origin. The IRI undertook a bond issue, and to stimulate sales it created a contest, the prizes of which would be new Giulietta cars. When Hruska heard of this he said, ''*Ma siamo matti*—we're crazy. The platform chassis is ready to go, but an immense amount of work remains to be done on perfecting the body structure.'' But the public commitment had already been made.

The body in question was that of the standard, mass-produced sedan. Hruska came up with an idea for saving the day: work with a specialist coach builder, run off a limited series of sports models, and use some of them as contest prizes. But the release of a sports model prior to that of its basic, more utilitarian parent, was unprecedented, and the IRI people rejected the proposal. Hruska liked it so well that he offered to quit and undertake the project himself, which would still provide the IRI with a way out of the impasse. Hruska could visualize the end product, which he knew would be a winner, and all he asked for his proposed services was exclusive sales rights for the sports model. Luraghi saved the situation by bringing the IRI around to acceptance of Hruska's original idea. He presented it to his friend Nuccio Bertone, and the Giulietta Sprint phenomenon was the result. The IRI had imagined a production run of 200 units, whereas the demand lasted for 11 years and absorbed 27,142 cars. At the request of his friend Max Hoffman of New York, Hruska laid the groundwork for the Giulietta Spider by Pininfarina. Fusi shows 17,290 of these to have been made.

Much of the development testing of the Giulietta in its various forms was done on weekends by Hruska, most of it on standard routes between Turin and the French Cote d'Azur, sharing the work with his wife or Consalvo Sanesi.

Alfasud sprint.

Hruska with Dr. Guiseppe Luraghi.

In 1956, Luraghi, in a dispute with certain elements in the IRI and Finmeccanica, resigned and took over the presidency of a giant textile firm, Lanerossi. In that same year, Hruska was advanced to the position of assistant managing director of Alfa, responsible for the technical, production, and economic sectors of the firm. His superior was Ing. Franceso Quaroni, managing director of Alfa since 1952, another product of the Pirelli organization and a close friend of Luraghi and Hruska. When Quaroni resigned from Alfa in 1959, Hruska decided that it was time for him, too, to move on.

Early in 1960 he signed a contract with Fiat. It made him a technical consultant in liaison between Fiat managing director Ing. Bono in Turin and Enrico Pigozzi, founder and president of Simca, in Paris. Much had been going on with the French company, which was largely a Fiat subsidiary. In 1954, it had bought the Ford France plant at Poissy and in 1958, Chrysler USA bought a 15 percent interest in Simca. Hruska came to know the Simca organization intimately. Following Pigozzi's death in 1964 Fiat sold the rest of Simca to Chrysler and rotated Hruska back to Turin. There he was put in charge of Fiat's entire program for cars of sporting character, of which the Dino was an outstanding example. It was a job which he really relished.

In the meanwhile, the bruised relations between Luraghi and the IRI and Finmeccanica had healed and in 1960 Luraghi took over as president of Alfa Romeo. Excellent friends that he and Hruska were, they remained in contact until one day in 1967, when Luraghi called Hruska to Milan. He told him, in effect:

> We here at Alfa Romeo have to set up an engineering company for the planning of an industrial enterprise. It is better that you don't know what it is at this time, but I can tell you that it is something that you will love to get your teeth into. Join us, and I will put you in charge of this new company. If the program doesn't work out, you will become managing director of Alfa Romeo, under me.

Hruska knew that Luraghi was a man of his word, and without too much hesitation he resigned from his position with Fiat. As he tells the story, Hruska reported to Luraghi in July 1967, to take over as the managing director of a company called Studi Impianti Consulenza Automobilistiche or, preferably, SICA. He learned that there was a very large car factory to be conceived and put on paper but that, first, the product itself had to be designed. It had to be a car that would enable Alfa to increase its annual sales from a ceiling of about 100,000 to one of between 300,000 and 350,000. To generate that volume the car would have to be much less expensive than the Giulia which was in production and the 1750 and 2000 which were just making their bow. The market segment to aim at clearly seemed to be the one then occupied by such vehicles as the Fiat 128 and the Opel Kadett. Luraghi gave Hruska an errand boy and a girl who could type. When he asked for competent technical personnel he was told that there was none to spare at Alfa and that he would have to solve that problem himself. The detailed preliminary studies of car and factory, including costs, would have to be submitted to the IRI in six months.

Rather than waste precious time looking for qualified help at this stage, Hruska plunged into the car project alone. He did a rapid analysis of the market segment in question and began to lay out his car on graph paper. Starting with the engine, he opted for a flat four, not because of his Porsche conditioning, he says, but to fit his concept of the vehicle to be. He visualized it as pertaining to the target segment in overall characteristics, but a notch above it in terms of interior space, comfort, silence, and performance. The boxer four would eliminate the vibrations normal to in-line fours, and thus contribute to silence, smoothness, and comfort. In passing, it would permit an aerodynamically desirable low hood line. Making the crankcase in cast iron rather than in aluminum would add other advantages, silence being the most obvious of them. Investing in such refinements as overhead camshafts and double valve springs would enhance specific output and be consistent with Alfa tradition. Hruska had the basic engine layout completed

The entrance to the factory at Portello in the Fifties.

within a month, at which time Luraghi sent him help in the person of Ing. Domenico Chirico, from the Alfa experimental department. Chirico studied the design and said that he could add nothing to it—it was already done. Hruska had already laid out the rest of what would be the Alfasud around this engine and had prepared tables of dimensions, the weight of individual components, the man-hours for bodywork and mechanicals, the cost of materials. When all this had been verified by Chirico, Hruska submitted it to Luraghi. He approved it, and gave Hruska the go-ahead to start hiring staff for the detailed, definitive design of the engine, and to make the preliminary studies for a new factory. With potential expansion in mind, it should have a production capacity of 1000 cars per day. This specification of course was perfectly tailored to Hruska's background.

With the purchase of Ford France, Simca had also acquired its staff and, with the help of this know-how, had arrived at a production of 1200 cars per day. And, very interestingly, those cars were more economical to build than Fiats were. When Chrysler bought Simca it installed its own executive personnel, letting the Ford executives go. Knowing all this from the inside, Hruska was able to hire the Ford-trained, ex-Simca directors of production, of organization, and of finance, among many others, to help with planning the factory. Ing. Carlo Chiti was borrowed from Alfa's racing branch, Autodelta, to do the definitive engine layout. Drawing the rest of the chassis was entrusted by Hruska to a Porsche engineer, Heinrich Hoffmann, and this whole equipe was in place and at work in October.

As soon as Luraghi had given the green light to hire, Hruska turned over his body sketches to Giorgetto Giugiaro, of Italdesign. One of the details of which Hruska considers himself the father was his pioneer high rear-end treatment, conceived to increase luggage capacity; Giugiaro, whom he had worked with during his Fiat *vetture sportive* period, had a selection of small-scale models ready in September. There was no time for making a full-scale model in plaster or clay, so Hruska had it done in polystyrene, which he counts as another first. When the last detail had been finalized, a definitive model was made in plasticene. It was presented to the brass of IRI and Finmeccanica on January 16, 1968, along with a dazzlingly detailed *cahier de charges* for the entire ''Project BETA'' vehicle line.

Submitted at the same time was the preliminary study for the factory, including sub-studies of investment, organization, outfitting, and structural plans. The site would be that of the former factory at Pomigliano d'Arco, and production was to begin in 1972. That the deadline was met was a spectacular achievement, since it normally took five years to create a new design and get it into production in an *already existing* plant. As was the case with the Giulietta, everything had been done right the first time and there were no hitches. Hruska feels that one of the reasons that everything ran so smoothly was that he only reported to one man, Luraghi, and never had any complications with the rest of Alfa Romeo or with the government bureaucracy. Among the memories that Hruska recalls with much-justified pride is that, when Project BETA was completed, out of the 240 million lire which he had asked for, he still had 20 million left to spend. And he says, "The prettiest thing in my career was being given the possibility, at exactly 30 years distance, of doing for the Italian government exactly the same job which my teacher, Porsche, had done for the German government."

At the present writing the Alfa 33, Fiat Tipo, and Lancia Y 10 are produced in Hruska's Pomigliano d'Arco plant.

With his part of the Alfasud project completed, in 1974 Hruska was placed in charge of design and experimentation for all products of the Alfa Romeo group. As noted, he retired in 1980, but remains astonishingly active. An Alfa executive told me:

> I have never known a person who knows the automobile so profoundly, really viscerally, as Hruska does. He knows it in all its aspects — design, production, organization, financing, management, testing, racing, body design and engineering and, of very great importance, the consumer's point of view. It is terribly rare that one person is able to understand the problem so all-inclusively. He possesses complete competence. He knows everything about Alfa, and we're a bit jealous, because he's not Italian. There were those who mocked his Alfasud in the beginning, but it proved to be a genuinely outstanding product."

FILIPPO SURACE

IN STATIC PHOTOS FILIPPO SURACE usually presents an image of serene calm which goes very well with his widespread reputation of being a particularly distinguished scientist. In the flesh, however, he is normally vivacious, ebullient, and bubbling over with wit and wisdom. His three decades at Alfa culminated in nine years as chief of all the then-large company's research and development operations, with their staff of as many as about 1350 highly skilled men. "The whole huge lot were marvelous friends," he recalls, with fond feeling. "But, being Italians and therefore individualists, made getting them to work as a harmonious team a hefty undertaking." He succeeded well at that, as he did at his main, underlying task, which was that of architecting a large mass of the scientific foundations for the rapidly growing company.

Surace was born in Reggio Calabria, one of the noted beauty spots of Southern Italy, on March 28, 1928. He came from a technical background, his father being a specialist in the laying and maintenance of submarine cables. He attended his city's Liceo Scientifico and then commuted by ferry to the University of Messina, a few miles away on the Sicilian coast, where he studied mechanical engineering for two years. The best engineering schools in Italy

1978 Guiletta 1.3/1.6.

1967 33-2 8C Periscopica, first of the great Tipo 33 cars.

at the time were the Polytechnics of Milan and Turin, with Pisa a respected runner-up. He chose Turin where, after three years, he received his engineering degree in 1953. Although aviation was one of his compelling interests, he did not select Turin for its famous aeronautics department, but for its celebrated general technical excellence. Interestingly enough, cars did not attract him particularly, but his graduation thesis was devoted to the automotive uses of gas turbines, held in store.

Surace's exceptional versatility includes talent as a research chemist and his job was in that field, under Nobel laureate Prof. Natta of the Montecatini corporation. In two years' time Surace was called up for his year of compulsory military service. As it drew to a close in 1955 he happened to hear of an enticing job opportunity at Alfa Romeo. His impressive credentials were found to be acceptable and he went to work at Il Portello the following February as an experimental technician specializing in the development of gasoline engines of new design. He was perfectly competent at this nuts-and-bolts sort of mechanical work, but it was no more than work for him. What his mentality was made really to come to grips with were advanced mathematics and the pure, abstract theory underlying the laws of physics including, of course, mechanics. He managed to begin to apply these disciplines to a high-performance variant of the Satta 1900 engine and the results were so fruitful that he received nothing but further encouragement.

Surace's department head and immediate boss was none other than engineer Giampaolo Garcea, who had gone to work under Amleto Bossi in 1934. As we have seen, Bossi's fraternal and paternal transmission of Alfa technical tradition to Garcea made an everlasting impression upon the young understudy. And Surace recalls how Garcea received him with the same open heart and willingness to share the wealth of his knowledge and talent. Along with being a master of the mechanical arts, Garcea also was a skilled graphic artist, gifted in fine pen and ink sketching and floral painting. Surace cannot forget Garcea's ability to take his little gold fountain pen and draw an engine part which was under discussion. Then, if required, he was capable of drawing the surrounding parts from memory, going on until he had drawn the entire engine, swiftly and without error. "'Wonderful' is a word that really fits the man," says Surace. But his approach to technology was the traditional experimental one: time-consuming and costly.

When Surace came to Alfa early in 1956 he had no automotive experience and no expert basis for the comparison of automotive firms and their products. But elementary facts spoke for themselves. The Fiat 1100s of the time were developing from 36 to 40 bhp. The slightly larger Alfa Giulietta TI was giving a willing 65 bhp, and with the change of a couple of carburetor jets it would yield 80 bhp. Expressed in terms of bhp per liter the difference was enormous, of the order of 62 versus 38. Surace recognized in the Alfa product line one which had been developed to a very high level almost entirely through experimental methods. He also saw very clearly, he felt, that the days of such admirable leadership were strictly numbered, soon to be overtaken by bigger, richer firms which could afford to fight experimental methods with more efficient scientific ones. The only way to continue to compete, grow, and sustain leadership, Surace maintained, was also by the adoption of the most advanced scientific and theoretical techniques. In its existing financial state Alfa simply did not have enough money to do all of the work that a basically

Above: The 33 TT 12, winner of the Championship of the World for Marques, 1975. Below: 1977 33 Turbo experimental car.

experimental approach required. He convinced Garcea that a major conversion to the theoretical approach was the only hope for the future. Satta also approved.

In 1958 Satta created a new research center, of which he put Garcea in charge. Garcea took Surace with him, making him his chief assistant in charge of theoretical research. Working as a team the two men developed myriad new ideas and products. One example is the work which they did on drum brakes at that period, mixing mechanical and theoretical approaches.

"By using much sophisticated theory and practice in unison we were able to explain *all* the phenomena which bear upon fade and vibrations. With the help of design chief Giuseppe Busso we developed the two-leading-shoe brake that we called the bikini, which was the solution to combating fade. And then we did the three-shoe brake that overcame vibration." Many experts pronounced these the finest drum brakes that the world had ever seen. Then pioneer Alfa mechanic and driver Giulio Ramponi brought the disc brake from England. Being better and less costly it put an end to the best drums that combined science and mechanics ever made.

Surace has the distinction of having introduced scientific computers at Alfa Romeo. He began by borrowing, with Garcea's aid, the use of the accounting department's electronic equipment after the staff had left for the day and on weekends. Surace knew well what the results would be and cheerfully put in long extra hours to produce them. He began with body design, in which his interest was equally strong in structure, styling, and aerodynamics. Through the rapid application of many thousands of simultaneous equations, a product that was super-scientific in every sense took form in time that was unimaginably short at Il Portello. The point was quickly made that research and development had no future without this essential electronic tooling.

A decisive factor in the scientification of Alfa Romeo came in 1966, when Garcea and Surace were invited to Detroit by the Big Three for a series of seminars. Included in the visit were tours of the engineering laboratories and proving grounds of Chrysler, Ford, and GM. Surace still rocks with laughter over the impact of that experience, and its contrast with what they knew in Europe. The overwhelming message was that science was an indispensable path to survival in the years ahead. As Alfa moved rapidly to act upon the message, Garcea was made full assistant to

Left: 1984 90 2.5. Below left: 1983 F.1 car. Below right: The 1978 experimental F.1 boxer engine.

Satta, while Surace in 1967 was placed in full command of both theoretical and experimental research and development for the entire company. His man in charge of theoretical R&D was engineer Gabriele Toti, while the huge experimental sector was headed by engineer Aldo Bassi. Surace feels that, under its new scientific orientation, the technological culture of R&D at Alfa was soon higher than ever had been achieved in Italy. For 10 years, starting in 1958, Surace also found the time to serve as a part-time instructor in the automotive engine department of the Milan Polytechnic.

Orazio Satta died in 1974 and in 1976 Surace inherited his position as chief engineer of the entire company, with Domenico Chirico as his top aide. Surace was responsible for every element of the firm's products, from the micro- to macroscopic, from exhaust note to body styling and interior finish. He was responsible for such an enormous mass of hardware — with appropriate delegation of authority of course — that he rarely speaks of his own involvement in any particular element of it. Hardware creeps into his conversation more or less by accident, not as a pretext for talking about himself, but to speak of equipment. For example, you ask if he has any particular interest in aviation, to discover that he would willingly talk about

Right: Carlo Chiti.
Below: Guiletta 81.

almost nothing else. You find that one of his most recent involvements was in the design of a turboprop reduction gear in a joint venture between Alfa and Rolls-Royce. It pleases him to have equipped it with automotive-type oil scavenging pumps.

Surace left Alfa in September of 1985, after having held a series of posts at the very summit of Alfa's engineering management. He moved on to take a top engineering position with Piaggio—"not with the aero division, unfortunately, but with the scooters." This came up as our Alfa 164 was buzzed in Milan traffic by a brand-new three-wheel Vespa camioncino, a mini-truck. Such machines have been rendering service for decades with two-stroke engines in the 175 cc range. "I designed that new little thing" Surace said, making conversation. "It uses a 50 cc engine. I made it in diesel form, too."

Obviously, it is the engineering challenge and not the size or type of machine which draws him. Since childhood he has built ever-more-scientific model airplanes. He does so today, maintaining contact with similar researchers all over the world. He uses only rubber-band drive. He considers it to be the most challenging.

Surace retired in 1989. He lives in central Milan, surrounded by countless alumni of the old school, and by friends. One, a constant companion, Carlo Chiti, lives almost next door.

DOMENICO CHIRICO

Chirico (pronounced **kee**-ree-co) and Surace have a great deal in common. Both men were born in the same year, in the same town. They went through the same school system and one married the other's sister. Both went to the same class at the University of Messina. Chirico, born in Reggio on June 11, 1928, also came from a mechanically oriented background. His father sold Lancia cars and young Domenico grew up with a familiar fondness for the Dilambdas, Augustas, and Ardeas which were current at the time. Following Messina, Chirico chose to work for his engineering degree at the Polytechnic of Milan. When Surace became an Alfista it was thanks to a job tip-off received from his brother-in-law. The two men are sufficiently alike in appearance to be brothers. Height and build, complexion, and salt-and-pepper hair are all about the same today. Domenico has a lively sense of humor, if not as rousing as Filippo's.

A high point of Chirico's education came during the fifth and final year of his technical studies, when he took the automotive engineering course given by the famous Antonio Fessia, former technical director of Fiat and then of Lancia. He credits the great man with having given much form and direction to his life.

With his new engineering degree in hand, Chirico passed directly from school to Il Portello in 1952. He joined the new ranks at about the same time as his lifelong friends to be, Carlo Chiti and Giotto Bizzarrini. For ten solid years he worked on industrial vehicles: trucks and buses. Then he was transferred to Nicolis, under whom he worked as chief of the industrial experimental department until 1959. Following that, he was rotated back to design. He loved his job as chief of truck and bus design, which he regarded as ''real'' engineers' work, including the fine-tuning of reliability and production costs. His realm was *autotelai*, a term sometimes used incorrectly to mean chassis with engine but in his case having the correct meaning of chassis without engine. Through Garcea, he also became a pupil of that great guru of Alfa experimental tradition, Bossi.

Loving his work though he did, it was in a sector of the business that was withering away. The whole thrust of the company was toward the mass-production of passenger cars and, as Giulietta followed 1900 and Giulia followed Giu-

Above: 1983 Alfa 33; below: 1990 Alfa 33.

Right: The engine for the six-cylinder 3.0 model 75. Below: The 75.

lietta, it was clear enough that the industrials were dying. So in 1962 young Chirico, age 34, respectfully requested a brief audience with the man whom he still calls The Great Satta. He explained his wish to become part of the main stream of company life. His credentials were such that Satta very quickly sent him back to Nicolis, second to him in charge of all experimental work. There he remained until 1967, a most fateful year.

What did Chirico do during those five years? "The nicest things you can imagine," he replies without hesitation today. "They say that one never forgets one's first love. Well, I forgot my trucks and trolley-busses with no regret at all. Before, I had had only the most limited experience with engines — the heart of the vehicle, after all. Now I worked entirely on passenger cars, and about 50 percent of my time was devoted to engines. I had entered a bright new world."

Chirico says that the car of this period which he remembers with the greatest pleasure was the Giulia Super. The original Guilia of 1962 was a berlina, a car having four to six seats as opposed to the coupé, which has seats only for two. Like typical Alfa berlinas up to that point, its engine was equipped with a single twin-throat side-draft carburetor, and in this case the 1570 cc four developed 92 bhp at 6000 rpm. The car was a distinct success with the buying public and it pointed the way to a market for an even more tempting version. Satta's planners decided that about 98 bhp should be just the right maximum output and the design team in question went off in search of the trifling six additional horses. But reworking the carburetor and respiratory tracts refused to produce results of the desired quality: five bhp were attained with effort, but with an unacceptable roughness which had not been present in the less-pushed original engine.

It happened that, since 1963, the company had been producing a Bertone-bodied coupé called the Giulia Sprint GT. It had what was regarded as a sports-type engine, with the

Left: 75 twin-spark 2.0 Alfa Romeo. Below: Chirico.

same 1570 cc displacement as the family sedan, but with *two* twin-throat carburetors. It was a happy combination that yielded a silken 106 bhp at the usual 6000 rpm. Someone—and Chirico was probably very much involved—had the daring idea of cutting the Gordion knot by simply detuning the hot engine, rather than struggle with the recalcitrant single-carb version. Thus was born the Giulia Super, which turned out to be a whole new breed of beast and enjoyed much well-deserved popularity between about 1965 and 1972. The difference of six peak horsepower bore on the insignificant, but the relative abundance of torque in the more generally used area of the rev range permitted, paradoxically, much improved acceleration and, with it, a higher final-drive ratio. The power train turned more slowly and the wear of parts was considerably reduced. For the first time Alfa Romeo offered an everyday berlina with a strictly sporting power plant. Chirico stresses that having a separate carburetor throat for each cylinder of a twin-cam engine permits big gains in overlap—*incrocio di distribuzione*, if you would like to know the Italian equivalent of that exotic term. And the greater overlap and its ram effect can provide very marked increases in torque output. ''It is the most important feature of Alfa Romeo engines,'' he says. ''Remember that! And it also is the most important thing for unburned hydrocarbons.''

Out of the key mutation which was the Giulia Super there was developed, in about 1967, the great modern Alfa 1750.

While this milestone was being sculpted, in 1966, Rudi Hruska returned to Alfa Romeo. He and Chirico were good friends from Hruska's first period of service with the firm, and when the Alfasud program was organized Chirico was chosen to fill the position of chief engineer of this project which verged on the incredible. It was a great and fantastic

Below: Chirico in 1975. Below Right, from top to bottom: Cutaway of the 164; the 164; the 33 1.8 TD.

adventure in many senses. Among them there was an entirely all-new car to design and a giant factory in which to build it, all to be done in a mere four years, including the start of production. To complicate matters immeasurably, it was Alfa's first front-wheel drive production car. The project effectively began in September of 1967, when Chirico assumed his new responsibilities. In June of 1972 all Alfasud dealers assembled at the humming new factory at Pomigliano d'Arco to inspect, drive, and begin to sell the first of the new cars. ''It was like building a new city,'' Chirico says. ''Like building Brazilia. You have nothing but blank sheets of paper to start with.'' It is no wonder that the men who did the job still glow with the memory of it.

The staff was really minuscule from 1966 through 1968. It began with Hruska, his secretary, Chirico and three or four draftsmen who worked with him. ''In 1968 we began with five technical people and by the end of the year we had managed to work our way up to 15. We can say that the car was born on the drawing board with the work of 10 to 15 men.

''Of course many others worked to create prototype parts at Il Portello and in outside establishments. It can be said that serious office work really got under way in December of 1967 and that it was exactly on the 14th of the following July that the first boxer engine ran on the test bench. And in November of that same year the first car ran under its own power on the test track at Balocco. It was truly an exceptional experience, building a car in a year, and it seems incredible today, as it even did then. But I think that you could still do it, with everything perfectly organized and bureaucracy cut to the barest essentials.''

Chirico is a very philosophical maestro of production. There is little room for sentiment if you want to get the job

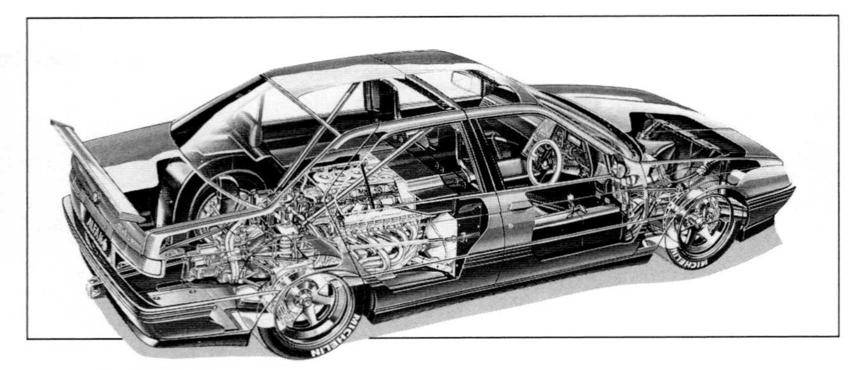

YEAR	RACE	LOCATION	DRIVER	PLACE	CAR TYPE
1934	G.P. Comminges	St. Gaudens, France	G. Comotti	I	2900 P3
1934	G.P. Casablanca	Anfa, Morocco	L. Chiron	I	P3
1934	G.P. de Nice	Nice	A. Varzi	I	2900 P3
1934	Targa Florio	Sicily	A. Varzi	I	2900 P3
1934	Circuito di Biella	Biella	C.F. Trossi	I	2900 P3
1934	G.P. Bordino	Alessandria	A. Varzi L. Chiron M. Tadini	I II III	2900 P3 2900 P3 8C 2600 M
1934	Coppa Ciano	Livorno	A. Varzi	I	2900 P3
1934	G.P. di Tripoli	Mellaha	A. Varzi G. Moll L. Chiron	I II III	2900 P3 2900 P3 2900 P3
1934	Avusrennen	Avus, Germany	G. Moll	I	3200 P3
1934	G.P. Penya Rhin	Montjuich, Spain	A. Varzi L. Chiron M. Lehoux	I II III	2900 P3 2900 P3 2900 P3
1934	G.P. de Monaco	Monaco	G. Moll	I	2900 P3
1934	G.P. de Montreux	Montreux, Switzerland	C.F. Trossi	I	2900 P3
1934	24 Heures du Mans	Le Mans	Chinetti-Etancelin	I	8C 2300
1934	Mille Miglia	Brescia	Varzi-Bignami Nuvolari-Siena Chiron-Rosa	I II III	8C 2600 M 8C 2300 M 8C 2600 M
1934	Targa Abruzzo	Pescara	Cortese-Severi Tadini-Barbieri Rosa-Comotti	I II III	6C 2300 6C 2300 6C 2300
1934	Stelvio Hill Climb	Stelvio	M. Tadini	I	8C 2600 M
1934	Parma-Berceto Hill Climb	Parma	N. Barbieri	I	8C 2600 M
1934	Mannin Moar	Isle of Man	B.E. Lewis	I	P3
1935	G.P. de Nice	Nice	T. Nuvolari L. Chiron R. Dreyfus	I II III	3500 P3 3200 P3 3200 P3
1935	G.P. de Lorraine	Seichamps, France	L. Chiron	I	3500 P3
1935	G.P. de Pau	Pau	T. Nuvolari	I	2900 P3
1935	G.P. de Dieppe	Dieppe	R. Dreyfus	I	3500 P3
1935	Targa Florio	Sicily	A. Brivio	I	2900 P3
1935	Coppa Ciano	Livorno	T. Nuvolari A. Brivio C.F. Trossi	I II III	3500 P3 3200 P3 3200 P3
1935	Circuito di Modena	Modena	T. Nuvolari M. Tadini C. Pintacuda	I II III	3500 P3 2900 P3 2900 P3
1936	G.P. Donington	Donington Park	H. Ruesch R. Seaman	I	8C
1936	Mille Miglia	Brescia	Brivio-Ongaro Farina-Meazza Pintacuda-Stefani	I II III	8C 2900 A 8C 2900 A 8C 2900 A
1936	G.P. de Belgique	Spa	Severi-Sommer	I	8C 2900 A
1937	G.P. di Milano	Milano	T. Nuvolari G. Farina H. Ruesch	I II III	12C 12C 12C
1937	Circuito di Torino	Torino	A. Brivio G. Farina C.F. Trossi	I II III	12C 12C 12C

YEAR	RACE	LOCATION	DRIVER	PLACE	CAR TYPE
1937	G.P. de Genova	Genoa	C.F. Trossi	I	12C
			M Tadini	II	12C
			E. Villoresi	III	12C
1937	Circuito di Napoli	Naples	G. Farina	I	12C
			C. Biondetti	II	12C
			E. Villoresi	III	12C
1937	G.P. des Frontieres	Chimay, Belgium	H. Ruesch	I	8C
1937	Mountain Championship	Brooklands	H. Ruesch	I	8C
1937	Mille Miglia	Brescia	Pintacuda-Mambelli	I	6C 2300
1937	Targa Abruzzo	Pescara	F. Cortese	I	6C 2300
			L. Salvi del Pero	II	6C 2300
			R. Balestrero	III	6C 2300
1937	Moncenisio Hill Climb	Mont Cenis	M. Tadini	I	8C 2900 B
			E. Siena	II	8C 2300 M
			"Ventidue"	III	8C 2300 M
1937	G.P. Rio de Janeiro	Gavea	C. Pintacuda	I	8C
1946	G.P. Bourgogne	Dijon, France	J.P. Wimille	I	308
1946	G.P. Perpignan	Perpignan	J.P. Wimille	I	308
1946	Circuito di Torino	Torino	A. Varzi	I	158
1946	G.P. des Nations	Geneva	G. Farina	I	158
			C.F. Trossi	II	158
			J.P. Wimille	III	158
1946	G.P. di Milano	Milano	C.F. Trossi	I	158
			A. Varzi	II	158
			C. Sanesi	III	158
1947	G.P. d'Italia	Milano	C.F. Trossi	I	158
			A. Varzi	II	158
			C. Sanesi	III	158
1947	G.P. di Bari	Bari	A. Varzi	I	158
			C. Sanesi	II	158
			R. Balestrero	III	8C 2300 M
1947	G.P. d'Europe	Spa	J.P. Wimille	I	158
			A. Varzi	II	158
			C.F. Trossi	III	158
1947	G.P. de Suisse	Bremgarten, Switzerland	J.P. Wimille	I	158
			A. Varzi	II	158
			C.F. Trossi	III	158
1947	G.P. de Rosario	Rosario, Argentina	A. Varzi	I	308
1947	Mille Miglia	Brescia	Biondetti-Romano	I	8C 2900
1948	G.P. de France	Reims	J.P. Wimille	I	158
			C. Sanesi	II	158
			A. Ascari	III	158
1948	G.P. d'Italia	Torino	J.P. Wimille	I	158
1948	G.P. di Monza	Monza	J.P. Wimille	I	158
			C.F. Trossi	II	158
			C. Sanesi	III	158
1948	G.P. d'Europe	Berne	C.F. Trossi	I	158
1948	G.P. Sao Paulo	Sao Paulo, Brazil	J.P. Wimille	I	308
1949	Coppa Acerbo	Pescara	F. Rol	I	6C 2500
1949	G.P. Argentina	Buenos Aires	O. Galvez	I	308
1950	G.P. de France	Reims	J.M. Fangio	I	158
1950	G.P. di San Remo	Ospedaletti	J.M. Fangio	I	158
1950	G.P. d'Italia	Monza	G. Farina	I	158

YEAR	RACE	LOCATION	DRIVER	PLACE	CAR TYPE
1950	Coppa Acerbo	Pescara	J.M. Fangio	I	158
1950	G.P. di Bari	Italy	G. Farina	I	158
1950	G.P. d'Europe	Silverstone	G. Farina L. Fagioli R. Parnell	I II III	158 158 158
1950	G.P. de Belgique	Spa	J.M. Fangio	I	158
1950	G.P. de Monaco	Monaco	J.M. Fangio	I	158
1950	G.P. of Switzerland	Bremgarten, Bern	G. Farina	I	158
1950	G.P. des Nations	Geneva	J.M. Fangio E. de Graffenried P. Taruffi	I II III	158 158 158
1950	International Trophy	Silverstone	G. Farina	I	158
1950	F1 World Championship		G. Farina	I	158
1951	G.P. of Switerland	Bremgarten, Bern	J.M. Fangio	I	159
1951	Tourist Trophy	Dundrod, Belfast	G. Farina	I	159
1951	G.P. de Belgique	Spa	G. Farina	I	159
1951	G.P. d'Europe	Reims	J.M. Fangio	I	159
1951	G.P. di Bari	Italy	J.M. Fangio	I	159
1951	G.P. de España	Barcelona	J.M. Fangio	I	159
1951	F1 World Championship		J.M. Fangio	I	159
1953	G.P. di Merano	Italy	J.M. Fangio	I	159
1967	Fleron	Belgium	T. Zeccoli	I	33/2
1967	Circuito del Mugello	Florence	Bianchi-Vaccarella-N. Galli	I	33/2
1968	Daytona 24 Hours	Florida	Vaccarella-Schutz	I	33/2
1968	1000 KM Nürburgring	Nürburgring	N. Galli-Giunti	I	33/2
1968	Circuito del Mugello	Florence	Bianchi-Vaccarella	I	33/2
1968	500 Km Imola	Italy	Vaccarella-Zeccoli Giunti-N. Galli Casoni-Bianchi	I II III	33/2 33/2 33/2
1968	24 Heures du Mans	Le Mans	Giunti-N.Galli Dini-Facetti Casoni-Riscaldi	I II III	33/2 33/2 33/2
Manufacturers World Championship for Sports Prototypes up to 2000 cc.				I	
1969	Coppa Cittá Enna	Pergusa	N. Vaccarella	I	33/2
1969	500 Km de Bahia	Bahia, Brazil	Fernandez-Pace	I	33/2
1969	3 hours of Rio	Rio de Janeiro	C. Pace	I	33/2
1969	Zeltweg	Austria	A. De Adamich	I	33/3
1970	Temporada	Argentina	De Adamich-Courage	I	33/3
1971	1000 Km Brands Hatch	England	A. De Adamich	I	33/3
1971	Watkins Glen 6 Hours	U. S. A.	De Adamich-Peterson	I	33/3
1971	Targa Florio	Sicily	Vaccarella-Hezemans	I	33/3
1974	1000 Km di Monza	Italy	Merzario-Andretti Stommelen-Ickx De Adamich-Facetti	I II III	33 TT 12 33 TT 12 33 TT 12
1975	1000 Km di Monza	Italy	Merzario-Laffite	I	33 TT 12
1975	1000 Km di Dijon	Dijon	Merzario-Laffite	I	33 TT 12
1975	Coppa Florio	Pergusa, Italy	Merzario-Mass	I	33 TT 12
1975	1000 Km Spa	Belgium	Pescarolo-Bell	I	33 TT 12
1975	1000 Km Nurburgring	Nürburgring	Merzario-Laffite	I	33 TT 12

YEAR	RACE	LOCATION	DRIVER	PLACE	CAR TYPE
1975	1000 Km	Zeltweg, Austria	Pescarolo-Bell	I	33 TT 12
1975	Watkins Glen 6 Hours	U. S. A.	Pescarolo-Bell	I	33 TT 12
1975	Targa Florio	Sicily	Vaccarella-Merzario	I	33 TT 12
1975	World Championship of Marques			I	33 TT 12
1977	500 Km Dijon	Dijon	Merzario-Jarier	I	33 SC 12
1977	500 Km di Monza	Monza	V. Brambilla	I	33 SC 12
1977	400 Km Vallelunga	Rome	V. Brambilla	I	33 SC 12
1977	Coppa Florio	Pergusa	A. Merzario	I	33 SC 12
1977	G.P. Portugal	Estoril	A. Merzario	I	33 SC 12
1977	500 Km Paul Ricard	Le Castellet, France	Merzario-Jarier	I	33 SC 12
1977	250 Km Imola	Imola	V. Brambilla	I	33 SC 12
1977	300 Km Salzburg	Austria	V. Brambilla	I	33 SC 12
1977	World Sports Car Championship			I	33 SC 12

Primary Source: Alfa Romeo Catalogue Raigonne 1910 - 1982; Automobilia, Milano: 1982.

Ascari

Borzacchini

Brilli Peri

ALFA'S HEROIC AGE IN RACING

As a Mecca for talent, no marque has attracted drivers, including those of the most brillant quality, as has Alfa Romeo. The attraction for them was a function of the mystique, which included the marque as a standard-bearer of national pride and honor—the precise role inherited by Alfa's offspring, Ferrari, in the 1950s.

ARCANGELI, Luigi—Born at Forli, near Ravenna in 1902. He first attracted attention in racing in 1928 by winning the Circuito di Senigallia race with a two-liter Bugatti. In late 1928 and throughout 1929 he established a good record with Talbot-Darracqs. In 1930, after driving a Maserati to 2nd place in the Tripoli GP and 1st in the GP of Rome, he moved to Alfa Romeo, winning the Circuito delle Tre Province and that of Senigallia. He was killed at Monza's Lesmo curve in 1931, driving a twin-engined Alfa Tipo A.

ASCARI, Antonio—Born at Moratica di Benferraro, Lombardia in 1888, a very few miles from the birthplace of Tazio Nuvolari. Began driving Fiats in competition in 1919, Alfas in 1920. After many victories, killed in French GP at Montlhery in 1925. He was the Alfa agent for all of Lombardia.

AVANZO, Baroness Maria Antonietta—Born at Contarina Veneta, in 1890. Drove a Packard Twelve racing car, the engine of which made a lasting impression upon Enzo Ferrari. Drove a wide variety of marques, including Alfa in the early Twenties. Died in Rome in 1977.

BENOIST, Robert—Born at Auffargis, near Versailles, in 1895. Famous for his exploits with Delage. When that marque withdrew from racing, he drove briefly for Alfa in 1928. Died at Buchenwald in 1944.

BIONDETTI, Clemente—Born at Burdduso, Sardinia in 1898. He began racing motorcycles in 1923 and moved to cars in 1927. Driving Alfas, Talbots and Maseratis he won the 1100 cc Italian Championship in 1929 and that for 1500 cc class in 1930. He joined the Alfa works team in 1936, finishing 8th in the Mille Miglia. In 1938 he drove an Alfa with 308 GP engine, winning and setting a record for the 1000-mile race which stood until 1953. He won that race again in 1947 for Alfa and in '48 and '49 for Ferrari. He retired in 1954.

BIRKIN, Sir Henry "Tim"—Born in Nottingham in 1896. One of the famous Bentley Boys. In 1931, with Earl Howe, won the Le Mans 24 Hours with an Alfa.

BONETTO, Felice—Born at Manerbio, Brescia in 1903. He began racing motorcycles in 1920 and cars in 1921. After a long apprenticeship he began driving a privately owned 2.6 liter Alfa P3 in 1933, placing 3rd in the Monza GP and winning the Mountain GP in Switzerland. He was absent from the racing scene until 1950, when he acquired an old Alfa with 12-cylinder engine, *drove* it to Portugal and, with no practice, won an important race there. In 1952 he *won* the Targa Florio with a modified Lancia Aurelia and in 1953 was killed in the Carrera Panamericana Mexico.

BORZACCHINI, Baconin Mario Umberto—Born at Terni in 1898. After a splendid career driving Maseratis, he switched to an Alfa 2.3 in 1932. He died in the same accident with Campari during the Monza GP of 1933.

BRILLI PERI, Gastone. A native of Florence, with a very brilliant career. He began racing bicycles, then motorcycles. He began racing cars in 1914 and became an Alfa team driver in 1925. His first victory for that marque was in a P2 in the Italian GP of 1925. He died in an accident during the Tripoli GP of 1930.

BRIVIO, Marchese Antonio— Born at Biella, Vercelli in 1905. He began racing 1924 and in about 1929 became an Alfista. His first important win was with Siena, in the 24 Hours of Spa in 1932, followed by victory in the Italian GP. He retired in 1952, after winning his category in the Mille Miglia.

CAMPARI, Giuseppe—Born at Lodi in 1892. He went to work as a mechanic in the original Alfa company shortly after its founding. He began driving for Alfa in 1920, initiating a legendary career. His first GP victory was at Lyon in 1924, in the new P2. An oil slick on the large banked curve at Monza cost him his life in 1933.

CARACCIOLA, Rudolf—Born at Remagen, Germany in 1901. He began driving in competition in 1922, quickly finding his place on the Mercedes factory team. In 1932, while Mercedes was inactive, he accepted a place on the Alfa works team, along with Nuvolari and Borzacchini, driving 2.3s and P3s. In one of the latter he won the German GP on the Nurburgring. He returned to Mercedes after having won the Italian GP, also in 1932. He retired in 1952 and died in 1959.

CHINETTI, Luigi—Born in Italy, joined Alfa in the early 1920s, where he worked with Jano and Ferrari. He won the 24 Hours of Le Mans for Alfa in 1932, with Sommer, and in 1934 with Etancelin. With Chiron he won the 24 Hours of Spa in 1933. He is one of the Alfa old guard who joined Ferrari after World War Two, becoming an importer for the USA and founder of NART: North American Racing Team.

CHIRON, Louis Alexandre—Born at Monte Carlo in 1899. He began racing in 1923 and maintained one of the highest reputations in world motor sport until he retired in 1955. Usually associated with Bugatti, he changed to Alfa in 1933, in which year he won three Grands Prix and the 24 Hours of Spa. In 1934 he won the French GP with a P3, against the new German challengers. His last year with Alfa was 1935, when he drove the Bimotore. He lived to a ripe age.

CORTESE, Franco—Born at Oggebbio, Novarra in 1903. Most of his more than 30 years in racing were spent with Alfa Romeo but he moved to Ferrari in 1947 to become that new marque's first test driver. He was most noted for his great ability in road events, such as the Mille Miglia, Targa Florio, and Targa Abruzzo. He holds the record for participation in the Mille Miglia: 21 events out of 24. He died in his sleep in 1986.

DE GRAFFENRIED, Baron Emanuel—He began racing in 1946 and became successful in GP racing with Maserati in 1948. He won two GP events in 1949 and in 1950 was given an Alfetta to drive in the GP of the Nations at Geneva, in which he finished 2nd to Fangio. He continued to drive for Alfa in 1951, until the firm withdrew from GP racing.

DE PAOLO, Peter—Born in the United States around 1900 and introduced to racing by his famous uncle, Ralph De Palma. After a quick rise to prominence he won the 500 miles of Indianapolis in 1925, driving a Duesenberg. He was offered an Alfa P2 to drive in the Italian GP that year, and with it he finished 5th. This was his only Alfa ride. He lived to a ripe age.

DUBONNET, André—Born in France in 1897, into the famous aperitif-making family. He became prominent in the motor racing world with his victory in the Coupe Boillot at Boulogne-sur-Mer in 1921, driving an Hispano-Suiza. He drove an Alfa briefly before retiring from competition in 1928.

ETANCELIN, Philippe—Born at Rouen, France in 1896. He raced actively from 1927 through 1953. He enjoyed being independent, and almost all of the cars that he raced he bought himself. An exception was when he teamed with Luigi Chinetti in 1934, to win the Le Mans 24 Hour with a 2.3 Alfa. This was his only notable ride with the marque.

EYSTON, George E. T.—Born in England in 1897 and most noted for his Land Speed Record achievements. Following Ramponi's win in an Alfa 1500 in the Essex Six Hour race at Brooklands in 1928, the team of Ivanowski and Eyston campaigned a similar car, prepared by Ramponi, in 1929. They finished 2nd in the 24 Hours of Spa, followed by Rigal-Zehender in another Alfa 1500. Eyston and his co-pilot placed 3rd in the 1929 Brooklands Double Twelve and 1st in class in the Brooklands Six Hours. Eyston lived to a ripe age.

FAGIOLI, Luigi—Born at Osimo, Ancona in 1898. A leading pilot of his day, he drove officially for Maserati, Mercedes, Auto Union, Lancia, and Alfa Romeo. With years of fine achievement behind him, Fagioli joined the Alfa team in mid-1933, replacing Nuvolari, who had transferred to Maserati. Driving a P3, Fagioli won over Nuvolari in the Italian GP and, with other wins became Italian National Champion that year. He left to drive for the Germans in 1934, but returned to Alfa in 1950, driving Alfettas splendidly until they ceased racing in 1951. He was killed the following year in a racing accident at Monaco.

FANGIO, Juan Manuel—Born at Balacre, Argentina in 1911, and one of the greatest drivers in all of motor racing history. In 20 years of competition activity he won over 100 races and five World Championships, four of which were consecutive. He won the 1951 Championship driving an Alfetta, after having missed winning it the year before by a few points. He still lives in Balacre.

FARINA, GIUSEPPE—Born in Turin in 1906, the son of Giovanni Farina, founder of the coachbuilding firm of Stabilimenti Farina. He acquired an Alfa 6C 1500 and began racing in 1930. In 1933 he beat Nuvolari in a race at Modena, becoming to some extent that great driver's protege. He possessed superb style as a driver. He won the Italian Championship in 1937, '39, and '50, as well as the World Championship in the latter year, always driving Alfas. He was killed in a banal road accident in 1966.

FERRARI, Enzo—Born near Modena in 1898. He began racing in 1919, joining the Alfa works team in 1920. Between then and 1931 he drove Alfas in approximately 39 events, in which he scored 10 firsts. He died in Modena in 1988. See chapter devoted to him.

Chiron

GUIDOTTI, Giovanbattista—Born at Bellagio, Como, in 1904. He became a test driver with Alfa in the early 1920s. His first race was the Cuneo-Colle della Maddelena in 1927, with Emilio Gola. He was best known for his performances in the Mille Miglia, his first being shared with Attilio Marinoni in 1928. In 1930 he and Nuvolari won the event. In 1932 he and Cortese finished 2nd in the 24 Hours of Le Mans. In the early postwar period he served as Alfa team manager.

HOWE, Earl—Born in England in 1884. He began racing Bugattis in the early 1920s. His most notable exploit with Alfa Romeo is his win in the 24 Hours of Le Mans, shared with Tim Birkin.

Moll

LURANI CERNUSCO, Count Dr. Ing. Giovanni—Johnny Lurani was born at Cernusco Lombardone, Como, in 1905. His many distractions in the automotive field include 65 class wins, many of them with Alfa Romeo cars. In his mid-80s today, he is active on various commissions of the FIA.

MINOIA, Fredinardo—Born in Milan in 1884. He began racing in 1906, when driving an Isotta Fraschini he beat 92 competitors in the Coppa Florio at Brescia. He began driving for Alfa in 1924, when he finished 4th in the Italian GP in a P2. Co-driving with Borzacchini in the 10-hour Italian GP of 1931 their Alfa Monza finished in 2nd place. He died in 1940.

MOLL, Guy—Born in Algeria in 1910, of French and Spanish parents. By 1932 he was competing in such events as the Marseille GP in a Bugatti. He was "discovered" and groomed by Enzo Ferrari and began driving Alfas in 1933, taking 3rd place in the Grands Prix of Marseille, Nice, and Comminges. In 1934 he duelled with Varzi and Chiron to win the Monaco GP, among other excellent performances. He was killed in a crash in the Coppa Acerbo in 1935.

Nuvolari

NUVOLARI, Tazio—Born at Casteldario, near Mantova, in 1892, and one of the very greatest drivers of all time. Books have been devoted to him, one excellent one by Lurani. He began racing motorcycles in 1920, already 28 years old. By 1923 he was racing cars as well, but it was not until he was 38, in 1930, that he obtained his first ride with Alfa, driving a 1750 in the Mille Miglia. The rest is history, of the most fantastic sort, as any reader of this book already knows. "Nuvola" drove his last race in 1950 and died of a long illness in Mantova three years later.

Pintacuda

Varzi

PINTACUDA, Carlo Mario—Italian, adherent of the Scuderia Ferrari. After winning the Tour of Italy in 1934 in a Lancia, he won the 1935 Mille Miglia in an Alfa shared with Alessandro Della Stufa. The following year he finished 3rd. In 1937 he won the Mille Miglia again, plus the GP of Rio de Janeiro, beating Stuck's Auto Union. In 1938 he repeated his Brazilian win, adding to it the 24 Hours of Spa and finishing 2nd in the Mille Miglia, all of this with Alfas. He died in Milan in 1972.

RAMPONI, Giulio—Born in Milan in 1902. He was a young neighbor of Campari and, at the driver's request, was hired by Alfa as an apprentice mechanic in October 1919. He served as a teenage riding mechanic with Campari, Ascari, and Ferrari in a host of races. He rode with Campari to win the 1928 Mille Miglia in an Alfa 1500. In the same year he himself drove a similar car to his first important victory, that of the Essex Six Hour race, at Brooklands. Rich in achievements, he opened his own Alfa maintenance center in London in the late Thirties. An Alfista to the end, he died in South Africa in 1986.

RIGAL, Louis—A Frenchman who began his racing career in 1922, driving for Aries and Peugeot. In 1930 he became a member of the Il Portello team, specializing in endurance races. His performance record was not particularly notable.

SANESI, Consalvo—Born at Arezzo in 1911. His entire career was spent with Alfa Romeo. He was a formidable test and race driver. See the section devoted to him under the heading of The Satta School, of which he was a part.

SIVOCCI, Ugo—Born in Italy. A former bicycle racer turned test and racing driver. Hired by Alfa Romeo in 1920, becoming part of the three-man works team which included Ascari and Campari. A good friend of Enzo Ferrari, who wrote that it was Sivocci who "opened the doors of Milan" to him, including those of Il Portello. Sivocci won the 1923 Targa Florio, driving an Alfa RL TF. He was killed at Monza in September of that year, while testing one of Merosi's P1 GP cars.

SOMMER, Raymond—Born in Paris in 1906. He began racing in 1928, soon establishing himself as one of France's greatest drivers. His most famous victories were his two consecutive wins at Le Mans, both driving the same Alfa 2.3. He shared the car in 1932 with Chinetti and in 1933 with Nuvolari. He continued to race until 1950 when, in a very minor event at Cadours, France, he crashed fatally due to mechanical failure.

TARUFFI, Piero—Born at Albano Laziale, near Rome, in 1906. A mechanical engineer and a master in various branches of motor racing. He began with motorcycles. His first car-racing victory was in the Tunis-Tripoli road race of 1930, driving an Alfa 1750. He raced both cars and motorcycles for the Scuderia Ferrari from 1931 through 1933, finishing 3rd in the Mille Miglia that year. Thereafter, his Alfa rides were infrequent: he drove the 308 and 312, then finished 4th in the Carrera Panamericana Mexico in an Alfa Freccia d'Oro. He retired as a driver in 1957 and died in Rome in 1988.

TROSSI, Count Carlo Felice—Born at Biella, Vercelli in 1908. He began his racing career in the late Twenties, driving supercharged Mercedes. He soon changed to Alfa Romeo and in 1932 he and Brivio finished 2nd in the Mille Miglia. In 1933 he won five races, was 3rd in the Monaco GP, and became president of the Scuderia Ferrari. Driving Alfettas, he won the 1947 Italian GP and in 1948 the Swiss GP. He died of cancer in Switzerland in 1949.

VARZI, Achille—Born in Galliate, Novarra in 1904. One of the phenomenal drivers of all time, and the habitual adversary of Nuvolari, with whom he fought spirited duals for years. In contrast to Nuvolari's dramatic driving, he drove with an icy calm. He began racing motorcycles in 1923, changing to cars in 1928. His performance with a Bugatti led Alfa to offer him a modified P2, with which he finished 2nd in the GP of Europe at Monza that year. From then on his performance was steadily brilliant, often legendary. He continued to forge the legend until June 1948 when, in practice for the Swiss GP at Bern, his Alfetta left the road, with fatal results for the driver.

WIMILLE, Jean-Pierre—Born in Paris in 1908. He began racing Bugattis in 1931, becoming a member of the factory team in 1934, soon rising to top international rank. He joined the official Alfa team in 1946, placing his 158 2nd at Geneva. He won the Coupe de Paris with an Alfa 3000. In 1947 he won the Swiss and Belgian Grands Prix with a 158. He then transferred to Gordini and in January 1949 was killed in a racing accident in Buenos Aires.

WAGNER, Louis—Born in France in 1882. A member of the Darracq team, he won the Circuit des Ardennes voiturette race in 1903. He moved to Fiat in 1907, winning the American Grand Prize race at Savannah in 1908. He continued to build an excellent racing record. In 1924 this veteran of the heroic age joined the Alfa team, placing 4th in the French GP and 2nd in the Italian GP, driving a P2. He retired in about 1928 and died in 1960.

ZEHENDER, Goffredo—Born in Reggio Calabria in 1901. This Italian with a German name is best known for his achievements with Maserati. In 1932 he campaigned independently an Alfa Tipo Monza, winning the Grands Prix of Comminges and Oran. He retired from racing and record-breaking in about 1938. He died in 1958.

BOOKS CONSULTED

Conoscere l'Alfa Romeo—Storia Strategia Struttura. Arese, 1983.
Alfieri, Bruno et al. *Alfa Romeo 164.* Milan, 1987.
Ibid. *Alfa Romeo Spider.* Milan, 1988.
Anselmi, Angelo Tito et al. *Alfa: immagini e percorsi 1910-1985.* Milan, 1985.
Ibid. *Alfa Romeo Giulietta.* Milan, 1985.
Bigazzi, Duccio. *Il Portello—Operai, tecnici e impreditori al'Alfa Romeo 1906-1926.* Milan, 1988.
Colombo, Gioachino. *Le Origini del Mito.* Rome, 1985.
Fusi, Luigi and Slater, Roy. *LA 6C 1750 Alfa Romeo.* Rome, London, 1968.
Fusi, Luigi. *Tuttle le Vetture Alfa Romeo dal 1910.* Milan, 1978.
Ibid. *Alfa Romeo—La Monoposto Tipo A del 1931.* Milan, 1982.
Ibid. et al. *Le Alfa Romeo di Vittorio Jano.* Milan, 1982.
Ibid. *Le Alfa Romeo di Merosi e di Romeo.* Gorgonzola, 1985.
Garcia, G. A. et al. *Alfa Romeo History Museum.* Arese, 1979.
Ibid. *Alfa Romeo 1900 Sprint.* Milan, 1983
Gobbato, Ing. Ugo. *Organizzazione dei Fattori della Produzione.* Turin, 1930.
Hull, Peter and Slater, Roy. *Alfa Romeo—a History.* London, 1964.
Lurani, Count G. et al. *Alfa Romeo—catalogue raisonné 1910-1982.* Milan, 1982
Minebri, Marcello. *Alfa Romeo—Zagato SZ, TZ.* Brescia, 1985.
Moore, Simon. *The Immortal 2.9* Seattle, 1986.
Moretti, Valerio. *Enzo Ferrari Pilota-Corse e vittorie del mago di Maranello.* Rome, 1987.
Owen, David. *Alfissimo! Alfa Romeo—1900, Giulietta, Giulia, Alfetta, New Giulietta.* London, 1979.
Ibid. *The Alfausud.* Croydon, 1985.
Schmidt, Giulio. *Le Corse Ruggenti-La Vera storia di Enzo Ferrari pilota.* Milan, 1988. Translated to English by Pietro Castiglioni, distributed by Automobile Quarterly.
Wilson, Evan. *Alfa Romeo Giulietta—750 and 101 series Giuliettas and Giulias; 1954-1965.* London, 1982.

ACKNOWLEDGEMENTS

The author wishes to express his appreciation to the following individuals, each of whom has made a valuable contribution to this book.

INTERVIEWS

Adolfo Bearzotti, Milan
Donatella Biffignandi, Turin
Duccio Bigazzi, Milan
Bruno Bonino, Milan
Giuseppe Busso, Arese
Carlo Chiti, Milan
Gioachino Colombo, Milan
Enzo Ferrari, Modena
Luigi Fusi, Milan
Giampaolo Garcea, Milan
Pierugo Gobbato, Turin
Rudolf Hruska, Turin
Vittorio Jano, Turin
Erwin Landsberg, Milan
Edo Masoni, Milan
Livio Nicolis, Milan
Renzo Parigi, Arese
Franco Perugia, Monza
Giulio Ramponi, London
José-Ramón Ricart, Barcelona
Consalvo Sanesi, Milan
Orazio Satta Puliga, Milan

DOCUMENTATION—Arese

Artemia Canella
Gabriella Cislaghi
Raimondo Corsi di Turri
Antonio Magro
Elvira Ruocco

MANAGEMENT EXTERNAL RELATIONS—Arese

Roberto Benvenuti
Mauro Coppini
Rinaldo Hercolani
Franco Massari
Alberto Scandolara

PRODUCTION CREDITS

All black-and-white photography is courtesy of the author, Alfa Romeo of North America or the Centro di Documentazione Storica Alfa Romeo. The only exception is on the back cover of dust jacket: Merosi's children (upper left), courtesy of Studio Anselmi. All color photography is the work of Roy D. Query, except the following: p. 20 and 79, Giorgio Boschetti; p. 141, Don Vorderman; p. 169, Stan Grayson; p. 176, middle right and bottom, Ross-Elhart. The photograph on the title page was taken by Brad Schaeffer. It was composed at the Raymond E. Holland Automotive Art Collection.

INDEX